Alan Bold wa[...]
attended university and trained as a journalist.
Since 1966 he has been a full-time writer and
visual artist and since 1975 he has lived in rural
Fife with his wife and daughter. He has published
many books of poetry including *To Find the
New*, *A Perpetual Motion Machine*, *The State of
the Nation* and *This Fine Day*. He has edited
The Penguin Book of Socialist Verse, *The
Martial Muse: Seven Centuries of War Poetry*,
The Cambridge Book of English Verse 1939–1975
and *Making Love: the Picador Book of Erotic
Verse*. He has also written critical books on
Thom Gunn and Ted Hughes, *George Mackay
Brown* and *The Ballad*. In addition he has had
many exhibitions of his 'Illuminated Poems'
(pictures combining an original poetic manuscript
with an illustrative composition).

The Bawdy Beautiful

The Sphere Book of Improper Verse

Edited by ALAN BOLD

SPHERE BOOKS LIMITED
30/32 Gray's Inn Road, London WC1X 8JL

First published by Sphere Books Ltd 1979

Introduction, Note on the Text and the arrangement of this
anthology copyright © 1979 by Alan Bold

TRADE
MARK

Set in Monotype Baskerville

Printed in Great Britain by
Hazell Watson & Viney Ltd
Aylesbury, Bucks

Contents

In deference to the anonymity of the poems and the
problematic chronology of some of them, they have
been arranged alphabetically without the definite
and indefinite articles. Detailed textual information
is provided in the individual headnotes and the Note
on the Text

Introduction

As sex is the most common of human factors it follows that sexually inspired verse should have a mass appeal. The potential is there; the public has been prevented from realising it. For four centuries the bawdy muse has been producing vigorous, impressive, endurable verse that has the interests of a large public at heart. However, social convention and antisocial legislation have combined, until comparatively recently, to keep this body of work from the general public, who still equate poetry with irrelevant metrical self-indulgence. Poetry proper has been progressively purified almost to the point of academic sterility and poets have been frozen out of the prevailing artistic climate. Those poets who have become household names owe their fame, or infamy, to extraliterary activities. Rupert Brooke, a limited talent, is appreciated as a sacrificial victim; Dylan Thomas, a great lyricist, is caricatured as a superdrunk whose very initials have an alcoholic ring. The public has been conditioned, schooled from childhood, to regard poetry as a peripheral phenomenon, a strange untouchable entity.

Yet if poetry proper has, by an arrogant indifference to people, brought neglect upon itself, improper poetry has been unfairly forced underground where it has put up with an uncomfortable existence. Still, in the towns and the countryside poetry – which is a grand description of memorable verse – has been written or orally composed for the edification of those with a fine appreciation of sexuality. This poetry deserves to come out into the open because of its social, historical, psychological and artistic importance; and, above all, because it is so genuinely enjoyable when the inhibitions are no longer in total control.

From 1882–98 Francis James Child published, in five volumes, an anthology of *The English and Scottish Popular Ballads* that took as its qualitative criterion the supposition that a given ballad should have enjoyed an oral circulation. Ideally Child would have wished each of his 305 ballads (with around a thousand variants) to have been uncontaminated by human hand before they were for ever fixed in print in his epic of scholarship. In his headnote to 'The Laily Worm and the Machrel of the Sea' (Child No. 36) he ecstatically pronounced it to be 'pure tradition, and has never been retouched by a pen'. That represented perfection for Child. In practice his search for the genuine oral article was elusive and he had to rely on printed texts, manuscripts, broadsides and correspondence for the making of his reputation as the supreme authority on balladry. Child did not collect his material in the field or the factory but consulted extant data and solicited contributions. What is good for balladry is better still for bawdry.

When I set out to collect material for this anthology of bawdry I realised that, like Child, I would be unable to gather personally all the poems and songs I wanted. I had no intention of tramping the countryside, tape-recorder in hand, to persuade folk to delve into their memories and sing their hearts out for a few pints. That is standard practice with modern folklorists who thus make private collections of what is basically public property. They mistake methodology for scholarship and see themselves as re-creative artists when they are simply reacting to a voice in the supposed wilderness. In the event they are as likely to receive something learned from print or even disc as an ancient text imbedded in the oral tradition. I make little meaningful distinction between urban printed bawdry and rural oral bawdry; both issue from the same human impulse. So when I set out to collect from the folk I had all sorts of folk in mind.

Accordingly I sent out a letter of appeal to newspapers and periodicals all over the English-speaking world. The response was overwhelming and about half of the poems in the anthology were collected from correspondents. Their spontaneous enthusiasm for the project was striking confirmation of the worth of my endeavour. Not only did I receive bawdry, some of it retained since adolescence; I also received advice and a good measure of anonymous abuse. One letter from South Africa is priceless as an example of the mentality that treats sex as a horrific spectre haunting the world. I quote it in full:

Dear Alan,
You are indeed *bold* to think that any decent South African will accede to your request to send you oral bawdry (i.e. filth).
If Britain has sunk to the gutter, and now grovels in filth, please do not think that we have. While your

government has legalised homosexual practices and mass abortion on demand, I am thankful to say that Rhodesia and South Africa have refused to sink that low.

I wish to remind you, kindly, that if you persist in your plan to publish filth (in the hope of making money) you will have one day to face the judgement of a holy God, and that you run the risk of the fires of hell after you die. I urge you to repent and seek the Lord before it is too late. Get on your knees in true repentance and pray 'God be merciful to me a sinner'. Please read Psalm 23 and Psalm 51, and turn to God. Surrender your life to Jesus Christ and start to follow Him.

I write as son of a Scot from Elgin who suffered for the faith of his fathers, and became a missionary in Africa. He led many thousands to turn from sin. It makes me sad that you, a fellow Scot, now want to write filth that will corrupt the minds and damn the souls of many.

God bless and save you.

Yours truly, &c.

That epistolary *cri de coeur* (in which the word 'filth' is lovingly reiterated) strengthened my conviction that it is time to present a sustained sequence of unexpurgated texts of bawdy poems. When people are left to imagine what these poems contain their minds will turn in acrobatic circles thinking the worst. When they actually see for themselves the earthy honesty of bawdry their minds will settle and their bodies relax. I am not claiming that bawdry has, as its creative priority, a therapeutic function; however, an honest appraisal of popular poetic sexuality may very well have a wholesome cathartic effect. Sex is perhaps the one vital element that transcends class and economic circumstance as it is gloriously capable of adding a magical dimension to any life. Bawdy poetry is produced by enthusiastic sexual activists and their attitude to the act itself has immense value; ignorance, in this area, is the denial of bliss. It seems ludicrous that while the mass consumption of printed and visual violence is tolerated as an integral part of life there is still a reluctance to accept sexual art as a salutary influence on society. I believe the individuals who created the bawdy poems were simply doing their fellow citizens a good turn and one good turn deserves another; in the context of bawdry this means giving the verse the benefit of the doubt. An empirically unbiased approach to the subject will provide its own rewards.

In citing the individual composition of bawdry I wish to dissociate myself from the tired old controversy between communalists and individualists that has so disfigured ballad-criticism. Elated by Jacob Grimm's insistence that *das Volk dichtet* (the folk make the poetry) scholars like Francis B. Gummere and George L. Kittredge conjectured that traditional balladry was originally created by a collective process during which a singing, dancing throng made an artistic commodity that was somehow more than the sum of its parts. Folk bawdry, like balladry, is in the first place the work of an individual. After it has been composed it alters in oral transmission sometimes for the better, more often for the worse. The anonymity of balladry is a consequence of historical circumstances. Some ballads are so old that the name of the creator has been sunk in the swamp of time. Yet there was also a time when folk productions, like ballads, were held to be the responsibility of the lower orders and therefore inferior to written poetry. Lord Hailes may have been creatively involved in the texts of 'Sir Patrick Spens' and 'Edward' he sent to Thomas Percy for inclusion in his *Reliques* but a respectable member of the Scottish legal profession was not willing to say so. It is a similar case with oral bawdry. With printed bawdry the anonymity is even more easily explained. When there was a possibility of social stigma, or even legal action, rebounding on the perpetrator of a bawdy poem, the creator of it was hardly encouraged to own up.

Discussing James Joyce's masterpiece, E. M. Forster declared that '*Ulysses* . . . is a dogged attempt to cover the universe with mud, an inverted Victorianism, an attempt to make grossness and dirt succeed where sweetness and light failed'.[1] For Forster, Joyce's transformation of Homer's *Odyssey* into the squalid one-day homecoming of Leopold Bloom reduced the epic to the level of the gutter. The same motivation informs much of bawdry. It is an attempt to portray sex in purely physical terms, to eschew the metaphysical apparatus that generations of poets have imposed on

1. E. M. Forster, *Aspects of the Novel*, London 1927, Pocket edn., p. 113.

a basically simple event. Bawdry deals with the act of love, not the art of romance. The popular tradition – the tradition that appeals to ordinary folk even when it was created by extraordinary people – has always been at odds with the rarefied offerings of art-poets. The man in the street whose instant comment on the pretty girl in the street is 'I'd be up that like a rat up a drainpipe' is not mentally attuned to exquisite wordplay. At its most refined, art-poetry has adhered to the conventions of courtly love. *Amour courtois* was perfected as a literary genre by the eleventh-century French troubadours. The elaborate rules of this game required the lady to be an unattainable goddess who contemptuously resisted the advances of the grovelling poet. As a contrast to this, the bawdy tradition usually makes the woman a more-than-willing partner in affairs of the body, almost always the easy victor in sexual contests. To this day conventional love poetry genuflects before the altar of courtly love so that the finished product is pure praise. Bawdry prefers pure filth to pure praise.

I remember as a child in Edinburgh – not so long ago, as I was born there in 1943 – speculating endlessly with my friends as to the mechanics of sex. It was something we were perpetually fascinated by and our ignorance intensified the interest. There was no sex education whatsoever at school and there were no books on the subject at home. We privately worried about our ignorance but, in company, tried to assert a nonchalant worldliness. Bawdry came as a blessed release from such emotional deprivation. On Sundays we would swagger childishly along Princes Street, look up at the castle that dominated the city skyline and chant in unison

> Edinburgh Castle stands on a rock;
> Every time you pass it you must show your cock.

None of us ever obeyed this injunction though there was a delicious taste of forbidden fruit once the salacious thought had been articulated. By 1956, when we had graduated to drape-suits and Elvis Presley records, we were not so innocent; still the pose of sneering super-sophistication could often be dropped in favour of a communal chorus of

> Antie Mary had a canary
> Up the leg o' her drawers;

> It wouldnae come doon for half-a-croon,
> It's still up the leg o' her drawers.

There was a local woman who fitted the description of Auntie Mary and we knew, intuitively, that the canary was a metaphor for the cock we were expected to flash before Edinburgh Castle. The laughter that doggerel instigated made us, I am sure, more sympathetic to the lady. Bawdry, at its most eloquent, is as reassuring as a warm bath and infinitely preferable to the cold shower of institutional ethics.

When I graduated from such elementary oral items to a systematic study of literature it always appalled me that the texts held up for critical examination were so far removed from what I took to be life as she is lived. It was inconceivable to turn from necking a bird in the local cinema and echo Shelley's words:

> One word is too often profaned
>   For me to profane it;
> One feeling too falsely disdained
>   For thee to disdain it;
> One hope is too like despair
>   For prudence to smother;
> And pity from thee more dear
>   Than that from another.

It was well-meant soporific stuff like that which put people off poetry for ever. School poetry-sessions are notorious for imposing the soppiest, most mendacious pap on minds hungry for an educated response to real problems. Even schoolteachers must realise sometimes that the words they regurgitate from set-texts have no relationship to the requirements of their pupils. University is more open but there poetic texts seem to exist solely as soft centres for sharp critics to sink their pointed teeth into. Whatever poets desire to the contrary, poetry is taught in such way as to make people suspicious of its intent. The further poetry moves away from the rhythm of speech the more pointless it appears. After all those misguided pedagogic efforts by teachers and lecturers the task of convincing the public that there is a lovely, lively human warmth to poetry assumes Sisyphean proportions.

Now I am not going to claim that all the work represented in this book is great poetry. Some of it is; some of it could

xiv

absolutely nauseate the self-consciously censorious sort who think that what is good for them is automatically good for the rest of us. All the poems, though, are honest expressions of sexual tolerance. This is verse that speaks for itself, that being the whole point of the popular tradition. This is verse that needs to make a public exhibition of itself. Not all the poems have originated orally but all of them have been either carried orally or at least whispered about from time to time. Their message has been sent out, surreptitiously, by word-of-mouth. I have tried to isolate a truly popular quality, have concentrated on poems with a broad appeal. This has meant omitting poems with erudite allusions, tiresome Latinisms, weary archaisms, awkward inversions, and contrived conceits. If the exhibits here presented are light years away from the multiple puns and metaphorical wizardry of an art-poet like Donne then that does not invalidate bawdry. It shows, rather, there is an honoured place for the enthusiastic amateur and this book is that place. So far this century bawdry has been mainly confined to period-anthologies aimed at scholars. Here bawdry is given back to the folk who created it, if they did but know it.

Where did bawdry come from, though? That is in some ways a rhetorical question. It came from the heated imagination of individuals who felt compelled to shape their fantasies into a memorable form: the more memorable, the greater the chance of survival. Sex has always been a favourite topic of conversation and the leap from conversation to poetry is only a matter of degrees of skill. If bawdry is as old as the human race then we know more about the chronological development of the word itself.

The noun *bawd* first appeared in print in William Langland's *Piers Plowman* (1362); one manuscript has *bawdstrot* (=boldstrut) which derives from the Old French *baudetrot*. A bawd was a procurer or pimp and after *c.*1700 it came to mean a procuress. Today the epithet *bawdy* has lost its prostitutional connotations and is synonymous with *ribald*. According to a leading authority on things bawdy[2] 'the oldest surviving erotic folksong in English' is 'A Talk of Ten Wives on their Husbands' Ware" (published, from the *c.*1460 Porkington manuscript, in F. J. Furnivall's *Jyl of Breyntford's Testament* in 1871). There is also an old ballad

2. Gershon Legman, *The Horn Book*, New York 1964, p. 414.

describing the relationship between Edward IV and the fifteenth-century folk heroine Elizabeth Lambert (alias 'Jane' Shore) – 'King Edward and Jane Shore' – in Ambrose Phillips's *A Collection of Old Ballads* (3 vols., 1723–5). It ends

> But brave King Edward, who before had gained nine victories,
> Was like a bond-slave fettered between Jane Shore's all-conquering thighs.

That is typical of the indigenous English popular tradition but, internationally, the literature of erotica stretches back centuries before the birth of Christ.[3] When we think of the written tradition of bawdry in English the putative father of English poetry, Geoffrey Chaucer, has a seminal presence: *The Canterbury Tales* (*c.* 1387) tell of more than a holy pilgrimage. In the sixteenth century, Shakespeare used bawdry with dramatic force and elegance and, appropriately enough, in a book on the bard we have a working definition of the subject:

> to be bawdy, a piece of talk or writing has to have behind it the intention to startle or shock. It also has to be at once more and less than sensual. Inasmuch as it labours the physical, it is sensual; but its other aspect is the exercise of wit, and this requires that the speaker remain partly at a distance from what he contemplates. Bawdy is often indirect, metaphorical or allusive. Only at its least subtle does it use blunt, unequivocal terms of sexual description, the familiar four-letter words.[4]

If that definition was accepted as the last word, a high percentage of the poems in this anthology would be condemned as unsubtle, for the desire to use four-letter words is rather compulsive. Bawdry, in fact, relies on good humour rather than ostentatious wit. Composers of bawdy poems are not out to impress their auditors as much as to entertain them. We can differentiate between erotic poetry and bawdy verse by saying that eroticism seeks to raise an erection while bawdry seeks to raise a laugh.

For the purposes of this book, which is designed for the

3. For an account of and selection from this international tradition, see my *Making Love: The Picador Book of Erotic Verse*, London 1978.

4. E. A. M. Colman, *The Dramatic Use of Bawdy in Shakespeare*, London 1974, p. 3.

needs of a large general public, bawdy verse really gets under way in the seventeenth century. Shakespeare had shaken the English language to its colloquial roots and the bawdy muse took advantage of this radical alteration of attitude to adopt a casual conversational voice as a substitute for the previous exalted singing tones. By 1649, through the bloody application of his theological principles, Cromwell was firmly established as the ruler of England. As his Latin Secretary he had the great John Milton whose *Areopagitica* (1644) had advocated a permissive approach to the printed word. After seven years of intermittent civil war the puritans were in a combative mood and their grimly disapproving attitude to fleshly pleasures provoked an inevitable reaction: bring on the bawdy muse! As a heartfelt contradiction of the official morality, bawdy anthologies, known as drolleries, began to appear – to the consternation of the government. *Musarum Deliciae*, the first of the drolleries, was issued by the publisher Henry Herringham in 1655. It was quickly followed by John Cotgrave's *Wits Interpreter* (1655), John Playford's *Wit and Drollery* (1656), and *Sportive Wit* (1656) compiled by Milton's nephew, John Philips. This was too much for the government who, on 25 April 1656, condemned *Sportive Wit* as 'scandalous, lascivious, scurrilous and profane'; all available copies were publicly burned by the hangman and John Philips was fined. Two weeks later, similar treatment was accorded to *Choyce Drollery* and the drolleries almost died out before they were resuscitated by the Restoration of 1660.

Although many of the poems in the drolleries have the familiar sound of popular bawdry they were not the work of the common man. Seventeenth-century anonymous bawdry, as a literary scholar of the period has pointed out, 'flourished among dons, lawyers, doctors, churchmen, country gentlemen, gallants and courtiers'.[5] The best bawdy pieces were, though, touched by the common love of sexuality. There was nothing gentlemen were fonder of than a quick bundle with the women they regarded as their social inferiors. For women it was rather more difficult to cross class boundaries. It is worth noting here that the proselytising Germaine Greer sees as one of the triumphs of women's liberation the possibility of females, like males in the past, consorting with those *they* regard as social inferiors:

5. John Wardroper, *Love and Drollery*, London 1969, p. ix.

> Rather than seek to be squired and dated by their rivals,
> why should it not be possible for women to find relaxa-
> tion and pleasure in the company of their 'inferiors'? . . .
> A learned woman cannot castrate a truck-driver like
> she can her intellectual rival because he has no exag-
> gerated respect for her bookish capabilities.[6]

In the seventeenth century, though, women were kept in
the background or confined to the bedroom and bawdry was
produced and consumed by men (Aphra Benn being, as
always, the exception). Post-Restoration drolleries satisfied
the masculine appetite for bawdy poems: John Playford's *An
Antidote Against Melancholoy* (1661) is typical of the eagerly
devoured collections. The drollery tradition came to a fitting
conclusion with *Wit and Mirth; or Pills to Purge Melancholy*
edited initially (1698–1706) by John Playford's son Henry,
and finally in six volumes (1719–20) by Thomas D'Urfey.
The king himself was a fan of bawdry: Addison wrote in *The
Guardian* of 28 May 1713, 'I myself remember King Charles
the Second leaning on Tom D'Urfey's shoulder more than
once, and humming over a song with him'. However, the
merry monarch was succeeded by the rigid regent James II,
with turbulent consequences for the country. There was a
glorious revolution, there was a parliamentary union, there
was a Jacobite uprising in Scotland, there was tension and
apprehension everywhere as well as increasing commercial
prosperity.

In 1724, a decade after George I had brought the House
of Hanover over to Britain, Allan Ramsay's *The Ever Green*
began the insidious custom of 'improving' bawdry by editorial
emasculation. Offensive words and phrases were quietly
deleted from amorous texts and the habit soon caught on. In
1744 John Wesley published his *Collection of Moral and Sacred
Poems* for the pure at heart; Thomas Percy's *Reliques of Ancient
Poetry* (1765) conveniently ignored the most bawdy pieces in
the celebrated manuscript; Oliver Goldsmith's anthology of
Poems for Young Ladies (1767) was suitably chaste; and in 1772
Bishop Richard Hurd brought out a castrated edition of
Cowley. All the movement towards literary purity needed was
a name. Harriet Bowdler's anonymously edited *Family*

6. Germaine Greer, *The Female Eunuch*, London 1970, Paladin edn.,
p. 319.

Shakespeare appeared in four volumes in 1807 and her brother Thomas proudly put the family name to the expanded ten-volume *Family Shakespeare* of 1818.[7] By 1836 the verb 'bowdlerise' had passed into common linguistic currency; the following year the Victorian age officially began with the accession of the eighteen-year-old queen.

With the development of self – and later state – censorship, bawdry went underground. Some of it flourished in the boozy atmosphere of men's convivial clubs. The Beggar's Benison club was founded in Anstruther, Fife, in 1739; the Crochallan Fencibles of Edinburgh was the club for whom Burns gathered the bawdry eventually printed as *The Merry Muses of Caledonia* in *c.* 1800. In the towns the broadside press issued sexual verse with relative impunity while in the country there were folk with memories good enough to hold and transmit poems orally. The only significant difference between the urban and rural bawdry was that the imagery of the former derived from adultery and naughty escapades whereas the imagery of the latter referred to agricultural rituals and natural rhythms. The townee regarded sex as a casual affair; the countryman saw it as a causal force. Artistically the difference between the urban and the rural poems was the usual distinction between a formal poem and an informal song. Beyond that the environmental matrix shaped the contents. As James Reeves puts it:

> A society which lives by manufacture and commerce is apt to forget its roots in the activities of the soil; the fertility of crops and herds is of no pressing concern. Human fertility alone becomes important. A city community, a town-dwelling and largely middle-class society whose relations are governed by politeness and restraint, takes human fertility for granted, and may even regard it as an inconvenience. Accordingly sex can become a joke, and the bawdy song may form the only recognised outlet for superfluous natural spirits ... to say that many folk songs have to do with sex is only a half-truth. It is nearer the truth to say that folk song stems from a civilisation, now long superseded in Britain, in which natural fertility was always a pressing and urgent concern.[8]

7. For a fascinating discussion of the impact of the Bowdler family see Noel Perrin, *Dr Bowdler's Legacy*, London 1970.
8. James Reeves, *The Everlasting Circle*, London 1960, p. 18.

After the restrictions of the eighteenth century, the nineteenth followed suit with more severity than sense. In the late Victorian age bawdry was a clandestine hole-in-the-corner phenomenon that was not to be spoken of in polite – that is, mixed – company. Yet the period experienced a prolific flow of bawdry, a torrential onslaught of new bawdy material. There were two reasons for this: the Elementary Education Act of 1870 helped to establish a newly literate mass audience capable of turning out ribald poems; and the emergence of Gilbert and Sullivan in the 1870s offered a popular style which could be easily parodied – as in 'Christopher Colombo' (No. 23) and 'The Bastard King of England' (No. 9) – or emulated.

Yet even this explosive resurgence of bawdry did not make the subject any easier to approach in print. When the pioneer of erotic bibliography, the businessman Henry Spencer Ashbee, compiled his first annotated catalogue of prohibited books, he used a pseudonym ('Pisanus Fraxi'), had the volume privately distributed, and claimed to have no interest at all in titillation. As he explained apologetically in a necrophiliac image:

> As little, it is my belief, will my book excite the passions of my readers, as would the naked body of a woman, extended on the dissecting table, produce concupiscence in the minds of the students assembled to witness an operation performed upon her.[9]

Ashbee's innovative courage was followed by the debut of the underground magazine *The Pearl* which was published in eighteen issues from July 1879 to December 1880. This situation meant that bawdy poetry had largely to be confined to all-male gatherings; had to flourish in bars, in army barracks, in prisons for men, in public (i.e. private) schools. These exclusively masculine institutions deprived bawdry of its great appeal to both sexes, and gave it a bad name as a sordid part of a man's world.

Although the Victorian age has been singled out as the most atrociously hypocritical period of our history it took the twentieth century some considerable time to shake off the Victorian hangover of sexual guilt. If bawdy or erotic books were printed they were packaged as expensive limited editions

9. Pisanus Fraxi, *Index Librorum Prohibitorum*, 1877, p. lxx ; the two subsequent volumes in Ashbee's trilogy are *Centuria Librorum Absconditorum* (1879) and *Catena Librorum Tacendorum* (1885).

well beyond the financial resources of the general public, who relied on cheap editions for their reading matter. Until the lifting of the ban on the unexpurgated *Lady Chatterley's Lover* in 1960, the majority of people just could not see their own everyday expressions in print. The censors thought they had a civic duty to protect shopgirls and factory workers from an anticipated deluge of unspeakable filth. Contrary to puritanical expectations Lawrence and Joyce and Miller have been enjoyably absorbed by the British people without any noticeable decline in moral standards.

In 1929 D. H. Lawrence wrote an essay on 'Pornography and Obscenity' in which he stated categorically

> Pornography is the attempt to insult sex, to do dirt on it . . . The only way to stop the terrible mental itch about sex is to come out quite simply and naturally into the open with it.[10]

Following Lawrence's example, most liberals have accepted obscenity while throwing up their hands in horror at pornography. The terminology of sex has become so confused that it is almost impossible for the ordinary reader to distinguish between the disgustingly pornographic and the endearingly obscene. If we take pornography in its literal sense – the portrayal of prostitutes – then much of the work in this book would be classed as pornographic. Prostitutes abound: Eskimo Nell is a whore as are Lulu, Charlotte and the various harlots of Winnipeg. Yet there is nothing stomach-churning about these girls, nothing that could be construed as doing grievous bodily harm to sex. If we accept the opinion of two American sexperts, then 'pornography deals almost exclusively with deviant moral or sexual behaviour'.[11] It is, I think, the practice of gloating over sexual abnormality that is repugnant to most people – myself included. The poems in this book all depict normal, natural sexuality; the use of outlandish hyperbole and caricature is wholesome, not horrendous. As demonstrated, though, some of the poems could be described as pornographic as a result of sheer semantic perplexity. Perhaps we need a new word to describe

10. D. H. Lawrence, *À Propos of Lady Chatterley's Lover and Other Essays*, Harmondsworth 1961, pp. 67 and 76.

11. John H. Gagnon and William Simon, *Sexual Conduct*, London 1973, p. 263.

the nastily impure; I suggest, instead of the etymologically maligned pornography, we use *carnography* (which suggests a desire to masticate flesh) to describe inhumane sexuality.

The content of the bawdy poems is, then, self-explanatory. Unlike the sensuous erotic poems of Ovid, Donne, Baudelaire and Lorca (to list a few masters of the art) they are not seductive; instead they relentlessly bump and grind their way to an orgasmic conclusion. Sex, in bawdry, is almost always a physiological trial and hardly ever a psychological torment. Stylistically the poems and songs could hardly be simpler. They invariably utilise obvious hand-me-down rhymes, except when suggestive rhymes are implied (see Nos. 35, 86, 115, 144). They rely on regular, thumping rhythms that crudely parallel the steady rhythm of the sexual act. The stanzaic patterns rarely depart from the couplet or quatrain and the tone ranges from a confidential whisper to a great shriek of delight. Bawdy poems are thematically predictable – boy meets girl; boy is had by girl – so the structural bond of the verse need only be sound enough to carry the undemanding narrative. For all that, the poems are admirably suited to their subject – for this is verse stripped of pretence and ready for action. Those whose primary interest in poetry revolves around euphony, diction, linguistic density and verbal texture will lament the paucity of dazzling effects in bawdry. Ribald poems are not static objects that need close critical attention; they are dynamic purposeful pieces of metrical machinery whose main purpose is to hold the reader or auditor in the grip of a racy narrative.

As such their appeal is timeless and classless. An excellent anecdote told by the Scottish novelist James Barke beautifully illustrates the point:

> It is typical of the Scots that when the Highland Division entered Tripoli after the success of the North African campaign, they paraded before Winston Churchill singing verses from 'The Ball o' Kirriemuir' in their lustiest voice. The broadcast recording of this historic event had subsequently to be scrapped. It is reported that, at first, Churchill was slightly puzzled by the song but soon broke into 'a broad grin'.[12]

12. Ed. James Barke and Sydney Goodsir Smith, *Robert Burns: The Merry Muses of Caledonia*, London 1965, Panther edn., p. 31.

The verses that Churchill grinned at have likewise entertained students and seamen, professors and postmen, businessmen and bartenders. And professional poets. I remember vividly a party held in Edinburgh, during 1970, for the late Robert Lowell – surely one of the most alert and sensitive of modern poets. A lot of strong drink had been consumed by one and all, and two revellers had Lowell cornered and he was clearly alarmed. When they began to regale him with 'The Ball of Kirriemuir' (No. 7) Lowell sat down and settled back to enjoy this impromptu example of popular Scottish culture. No doubt he thought this was a typical night in Scotland.

Of course it was nothing of the kind. Modern folk have been conditioned from the cradle to be discreet and it takes the de-inhibiting influence of strong drink to bring bawdry fully into the open. Often the enjoyment of it has the near-hysterical euphoria that accompanies the revelation of a well-kept secret. Bawdy verse champions the appreciation of sex as the basic satisfaction of an animal appetite and we are, all of us, proud enough of our evolutionary distance from the animals to feel embarrassed at a hearty reminder of our origins. We still act like apes trying to be angels. So sometimes we are ashamed of the sexual impulse, at least in the company of the opposite sex. We all know that bawdry exists but it simply reinforces the guilty conscience when it has to be acquired under the counter or within virginal envelopes delivered by the unsuspecting postman. For decades some of the finest bawdy poems have floated around in the oral atmosphere like ghosts that will only materialise when the human company is sufficiently fortified by spirits of the liquid variety.

As additional evidence of the unnecessary guilt associated with the enjoyment of bawdry there is the fond desire on the part of the credulous to attribute hitherto unprintable poems to great exponents of the printed word. The syllogism follows this logic: Shakespeare was a good man; Shakespeare was bawdy; *ergo*, good men are bawdy. Thus 'The Bride's Letter' (No. 17) has been credited to Byron, 'The Bastard King of England' (No. 9) to Rudyard Kipling, 'Eskimo Nell' (No. 39) to Noel Coward, 'The Heroes' (No. 51) to A. P. Herbert. The quest for respectable names to attach to bawdry has even resulted in the apocryphal *Sod's Opera* being touted as a work by Gilbert and Sullivan although such an authority as Gershon Legman has assured us 'there is no such work in existence as *The Sod's Opera* and never was'.[13] The exceptional achievement of poems like 'Eskimo Nell' (No. 39) and 'Abdul Abul Bul Amir' (No 1) need not be qualified; anonymous though they are, they sharply demonstrate the creative capacities of ordinary folk when fired by a theme they can warm to. At its most elementary this talent is seen in the ability of football fans to parody popsongs so that meretricious phrases become athletic slogans. At an intermediary level this ability results in the limerick, which is the vulgar equivalent of the short narrative poem. At its most advanced this gift creates the best pieces in this book.

Some of the best poems contain an inordinate amount of sexual boasting. This is a direct result of their genesis. Balladry was transmitted by women; bawdry possessed by men. In John Barbour's great fourteenth-century vernacular epic *The Brus*, the poet refers to a ballad like this (xvi, 521–2):

> Young women when they will play,
> Sing it among them ilka day

while in Shakespeare's *Twelfth Night* (1.iv) the Duke requests an old song, adding

> The spinsters and the knitters in the sun,
> And the free maids, that weave their thread with bones,
> Do use to chant it.

The most reliable provider of ballad-texts was a woman – Mrs Brown of Falkland (1747–1810) – who preserved thirty-three ballads (with variants) all of them canonised by Child. On the other hand there is a total lack of female providers of bawdy texts, though many of the poems were written – for the sake of piquancy – from the female point of view. In sexual matters women are doers rather than boasters and the fuck-and-tell mentality of bawdry is almost certain proof that *all* the poems and songs were, in the first place, masculine attempts at wish-fulfilment or displays of sheer admiration for the sexual capacity of women.

The explicit sexual data communicated in bawdry has, in my opinion, a real educational value. A knowledge of the bawdy classics is more likely to dignify sex than degrade it,

13. Gershon Legman, *op. cit.*, p. 96.

for the act of love is perfectly able to stand comparison with metrical descriptions of its power. The man or woman who gets married or permanently hitched thinking that intercourse will always be a bed of roses rather than an occasional pool of sweat is in for a disappointment. Equipped with a working knowledge of bawdry the same man or woman will approach intercourse with realistic expectations.

Moreover the poems provide an accurate picture of male fantasies and it as well for any self-respecting woman to take cognisance of these. There are, unfortunately, those who would deny the value of bawdry on the grounds that it could possible corrupt the young and innocent. I emphatically refute this suggestion because I believe that sexual knowledge is infinitely preferable to sexual ignorance. The young (I respect the legal age of consent and confine my remarks to those who have attained it) are sexually inquisitive and their problems are not always solved by the family doctor or the immediate family. Bawdry affirms that sex can be fun and that is a useful antidote to excessive gravity.

That egregious Aunt Sally of the establishment, Mrs Mary Whitehouse, utters her pronouncements on sex with an air of infallibility. This is what she has to say about the young:

> Subconsciously they learn that the peak of civilised communication is reached with the obscenity of the 'four-letter word'. No longer any need to enrich one's vocabulary with poetry, with great literature. No longer does society encourage the young to reach out to new dimensions of expression, rather do middle-aged intellectuals go down to join the adolescents in *their* culture, giving it the glow of the ultimate . . . Nothing, I think, more clearly demonstrates the sickness of the permissive society. It is not the conjunction of four letters that matters – ugly though the sound is – it is the reaction into immaturity, the glorification of the unlovely, which is so important. The betrayal of a generation which stinks in the nostrils.[14]

Apart from the painful prose style – which suggests more hours spent in front of the television set than in perusing 'poetry . . . great literature' – Mrs Whitehouse is implying that the culture of the young is intrinsically wrong. An interest in

14. Mary Whitehouse, *Whatever happened to sex?*, Hove 1977, p. 197.

sex and four-letter words is something they are expected to grow out of, as if youth was a pathological condition. It is as if Mrs Whitehouse wanted all children to be born as staid middle-class matrons or patrons so that adolescence could be eliminated, and all citizens could be left to their impenetrable prejudices. I think it is the moralistic denial of natural instincts that is ethically dubious. In passing we might ask why the sound of the four-letter word is considered to be so ugly. 'Cunt' is regarded as unlovely while the word 'country', which contains it, is the word for all things bright and beautiful. Even Shakespeare, hypersensitive to verbal sound, exploited the similarity of the two words in the erotic exchange between Hamlet and Ophelia in *Hamlet* (iii. ii):

> Do you think I meant country matters? *I think nothing my lord.* That's a fair thought to lie between maid's legs. *What is, my lord?* Nothing.

In D'Urfey's *Pills* there is a song 'Dunmore Kate' with the couplet

> She kissed his lordship o'er and o'er
> And opened all her country store

I think we have reached a sufficient level of social maturity to let all people, young and old, choose for themselves what they want in the way of entertainment. We have the advantage over our ancestors that there are more opportunities to savour all the varieties of artistic expression. Hence we are not so easily shocked by mere novelty. Even so distinguished an ancestor as Byron could be startled when he came across the bawdy side of Burns. In his *Journal* of 13 December 1813 he noted:

> Allen [i.e. John Allen, MD, 1771–1843] ... has lent me a quantity of Burns's unpublished and never-to-be published Letters. They are full of oaths and obscene songs. What an antithetical mind! – tenderness, roughness – delicacy, coarseness – sentiment, sensuality – soaring and grovelling, dirty and deity – all mixed up in that one compound of inspired clay!
> It seems strange; a true voluptuary will never abandon his mind to the grossness of reality. It is by exalting the earthly, the material, the *physique* of our pleasures, by

veiling these ideas, by forgetting them altogether, or, at least, never naming them hardly to one's self, that we alone can prevent them from disgusting.

The observation on Burns's contradictory character could probably be applied to all of us; the argument in favour of cosmetically tarting up sex is curiously coy. In *Don Juan* (1819–24) Byron was hilarious on the subject of sex. When it came to personal expressions of desire he lapsed into the platitudes of courtly love. However 'gross' he might be in his private life his public image, as revealed in his poems, had to conform to the highest aspirations of the Romantic movement.

As the Romantic movement was partly created by the publication of Percy's *Reliques* of 1765 it is interesting that the prime movers of Romanticism (like Wordsworth and Coleridge) tried to model their work on what they took to be the pure, chaste simplicity of traditional poetry. What was not known – until J. W. Hales and F. J. Furnivall edited Percy's Folio manuscript in 1867 – was that Percy had disposed of the bawdry. So the Romantic movement was based on an incomplete knowledge of the real situation, taking as its precedent fakelore instead of folklore. When the popular voice grated against the ears of the scholar it was to be silenced. It is this suppression of the truth that is so iniquitous and the fact that it continued for so long is unforgivable. Sabine Baring-Gould notating folksongs around Dartmoor in 1887; Cecil Sharp investigating the living traditions of song in Somerset in 1904; George B. Gardiner exploring orality in Hampshire in 1905 – they all expurgated their material so that the potent voice of the people became an emasculated falsetto. The rural bawdy song – hopelessly at the mercy of scholars – was doctored (i.e. neutered) before being pronounced fit for public consumption.

While the printed sources used in this anthology can easily be rescued from oblivion, folksong still has a reputation to recover. Country people were not insubstantial pastoral creatures but men and women much concerned with the flesh. Folksong has been badly served by its own addicts, whose snobbery has disfigured the thing they claim to love. In an essay on 'Pop Song, The Manipulated Ritual', folk-fan Charles Parker (no relation to the great virtuoso of modern jazz) compared the song 'Never Wed an Old Man' (No. 77) with Chuck Berry's number one hit of 1972 'My ding-a-ling':

> Now why should I find a rich and genuine hilarity in a folk club singing the chorus of the first song, and a sick and tawdry degeneracy in teenage fans singing the chorus of the second . . .? The answer, I submit, is because in the one, my response to the erotic implications is directed to a manifest social purpose – confrontation with the social injustice of wealthy old men marrying nubile young girls . . . In the second, my response is essentially narcissistic, masturbatory almost . . . and I am being titillated so that Mr Chuck Berry can get another number in the Top Twenty.[15]

I regard that outburst against popular taste as pretentious bullshit, an expression of the museum-mentality which believes that anything that has ceased to be popular is fair game for scholars while something that is still alive is bad, commercial, reprehensible, *et* bloody*cetera*. Too many scholars prefer to dissect the corpse of popular culture instead of handling the living body. I can see a future scholar drooling over Chuck Berry's song once it has been safely discarded by the fans; and despairing over some contemporary entry in the charts. Such a flagrant disregard for the judgement of the man/woman in the street has led the general public to associate folk music with fakelorists and to give the whole thing the thumbs down, a reaction that could be summed up as *Folk Off, Rock On*.

I hope bawdry never becomes so academically ultra-respectable that it can be dismissed in the same way; it should be studied, yes, but not confined to students. This book is necessary because I want the public to see what they miss when they reject poetry altogether. Perhaps, as a result, the bawdy tradition will get a new impetus. I hope so. I cannot pretend I derive equal enjoyment from every item in the book but it would have been an abuse of editorial privilege to exclude all items that were not entirely to my taste. The 144 (plus variants) pieces in the following pages could be described as the best pubic verse ever offered to the public. I have selected from drolleries, from once-prohibited books, from manuscripts, and from the oral tradition (with more than a

15. Ed. Peter Abbs, *The Black Rainbow*, London 1975, p. 164.

little help from correspondents). The cumulative effect of the poems on me has been to promote admiration for the anonymous bards of bawdry and to experience regret that their work has been kept from the public for so long. I hope, finally, that the book will help us look at ourselves in a realistic way as well as showing what bawdy verse is actually made of. Most readers, I suspect, will be in for a surprise.

ALAN BOLD

1. Abdul Abul Bul Amir

The Crimean War of 1854–6 produced William Russell's classic war reports, Florence Nightingale's nursing innovations, and Tennyson's 'The Charge of the Light Brigade'. It also inspired a harmless piece of metrical exotica describing a fight-to-the-death between young Ivan and old Abdul. By the 1880s this was ripe for parody and the man-to-man combat became a memorable sexual contest.

Now the sons of the Prophet were randy and bold,
Not scared of the dread gonorrhea;
And the randiest far in the ranks of the Shah
Was Abdul Abul Bul Amir.

Horny heroes were common and well known to fame
In the ranks that were kept by the Czar,
But the best at the game was a man by the name
Of Ivan Skavinsky Skavar.

Once a travelling brothel had come to the town
Which attracted the rams from afar,
And the foremost of them that so constantly came
Were Abdul and Ivan Skavar.

One night this bold Russian had bathed it in rum,
Then powdered his fine grinding gear;
Down town he did go, where he pissed on the toe
Of Abdul Abul Bul Amir.

For it happened like this, both had gone for a piss
Being full of the strong local beer;
And the spray from his root spattered on the left boot
Of Abdul Abul Bul Amir.

Quoth Abdul, 'My friend, I don't wish to offend
But this really is going too far.
You're not only a Jew but you're cut on the skew
Mister Ivan Skavinsky Skavar!'

Said Ivan, 'You git, you despicable shit,
You should not have been standing so near;
There's a stall up the end meant for kiddies, my friend,
Mister Abdul Abul Bul Amir.'

So this bold Mamaluke shook the piss from his boot
With a cry of '*Allah Akbar!*
I've ten roubles to bet I'll fuck more than you yet
Mister Ivan Skavinsky Skavar!'

To the race bounded they where the brothel train lay
And for once did not pause at the bar
But explained to the Dame the rules of the game
Between Abdul and Ivan Skavar.

She kept whores of all sorts, some tall and some short,
And a choice of young boys for the queer;
So with giggles and screams they all formed in two teams
Before Ivan and Abdul Amir.

When the word got about all the town tumbled out
To bet on the winner and cheer,
And soon multitudes came so great was the fame
Of Ivan and Abdul Amir.

They fucked several women, they buggered some boys,
And Abdul's arse revved like a car;
But most felt he'd no hope 'gainst the slow steady stroke
Of Ivan Skavinsky Skavar.

When the score reached eight–eight the Madam did state,
'We cannot stay much longer I fear,
Since they're both out of juice, why not now call a truce
Between Ivan and Abdul Amir?'

Neither one would admit he was no longer fit,
Each claimed he could fuck for a year.
'Bring on lemons or lime, this is only half-time,'
Shouted Abdul Abul Bul Amir.

But the Madam cried 'No!' – the train had to go,
She had bookings next day from the Czar,

2

And she could not afford to have all her staff floored
By Abdul and Ivan Skavar.

Though they begged her to stay she would have no delay
And locked all her staff in the car;
As the train rumbled out you could hear bookies shout
It was odds on young Ivan Skavar.

As he stood on the track with his tool hanging slack
He thought no defence for his rear;
He felt something hot whistle straight up his bot,
It was Abdul Abul Bul Amir!

And the cream of the joke when at last they were broke –
It was laughed at for years by the Czar –
Old Abdul the fool left the flange of his tool
Up the ringpiece of Ivan Skavar!

A vast monolith stands where the Blue Danube flows
And inscribed there in characters clear:
'O stranger when passing remember the tool
Of Abdul Abul Bul Amir.'

By the bank of the Volga, they tell me, at night
Ghostly screams can be heard from afar
As dead surgeons of class try to ream out the arse
Of the ghost of young Ivan Skavar.

3

2. Ainster lassie and her Creel

Ainster is the popular abbreviated form of Anstruther, a fishing village in Fife, where in 1739 the Beggar's Benison club was founded so that selected menfolk could sequester themselves and indulge in such activities as penis-comparison, drinking, ogling naked girls, singing and poetry-reading. Naturally the poems, like the following, were of a suitably bawdy nature.

As ae day Bob a fishin' gaed frae Ainster to Pittenweem,
A sicht! A buxom wench sat bent west by the Milton stream!
Wi' snickerin' host he frichted her. 'My lass! jist tak' yer
    time,'
When up she sprang as if got shot, like a poacher catch'd for
    crime.

The sun was hot, the burn was prime, so Bob jogged on his
    way,
When by and bye he peckish got and faiked amang the hay.
Syne farther up the Dreel he gaed, and cuist his line again,
But by some awkward management it hankered on a stane.

The Ainster lass was comin' back – by bad luck chance she
    fell,
An' drookit a' her dudds, e'en ane you guess, I sall not tell,
Whan she got oot – 'Laddie,' cried she, 'didna ye jist see
A fishin' creel o' curly wurly mak' – which belongs to me?'

The bluid ran boilin' thro' Bob's veins, when viewin' a' her
    charms,
He gently led her to the bank – she plumpt into his arms:
'Oh! dear laddie,' she said, 'what's, what's this trout I feel?'
'Haud it fast, my bonnie lass, – it's a fine big silver eel.'

'I hav't a' richt, it's deid, it's stiff, and yet it's warm as jeel;
To keep it safe, I'll put it in my ain guid curly creel:
There noo – whessht, it lifts – there's life in't yet – I feel,
For I fin' its heid aye dintin' on the bottom o' my creel.

4

Frisk aboot, my lithesome eel, as lively as anither,
Ye canna burst my midleg pouch, it's made o' ravin' leather.
Oh! laddie,' she cried and sighed, 'he's deid, my puir eel—
He's knockit oot a' his brains 'gainst the bottom o' my creel.'

3. Answer

Years before Beaumarchais's *Le Mariage de Figaro* (1778) made it artistically fashionable for employees to outwit employers this indigenous British broadside of c. 1705 portrayed a far-from-servile servant.

My lady's coachman John, being married to her maid,
Her ladyship did hear on't, and to him thus she said,
And to him thus she said:
   'I never had a wench so handsome in my life;
   I prithee therefore tell me,
   I prithee therefore tell me,
   How got you such a wife,'
   John stared her in the face,
   And answered very blunt,
   'E'en as my Lord got you.'
   'How's that?' 'Why by the cunt.'

4. As I cam o'er the Cairney Mount

In a letter of September 1793 Burns referred to this 'old humorous bawdy song' – to the tune of 'Highland Laddie' – and modelled his fine song of the same name on this coarse original. It was included in the c. 1800 edition of *MMC*.

As I cam o'er the Cairney mount,
   And down amang the blooming heather,
The Highland laddie drew his durk
   And sheathed it in my wanton leather.
   O my bonnie, bonnie Highland lad,
   My handsome, charming Highland laddie;
   When I am sick and like to die,
   He'll row me in his Highland plaiddie.

With me he played his warlike pranks,
   And on me boldly did adventure,
He did attack me on both flanks,
   And pushed me fiercely in the centre.
   O my, &c.

A furious battle then began,
   Wi' equal courage and desire,
Although he struck me three to one,
   I stood my ground and received his fire.
   O my, &c.

But our ammunition being spent,
   And we quite out o' breath an' sweating,
We did agree with ae consent,
   To fight it out at the next meeting.
   O my, &c.

5. As I was Riding

When Thomas Percy (Bishop of Dromore from 1782) prepared his seventeenth-century Folio manuscript for publication as the *Reliques of Ancient English Poetry* (1765) he deleted many bawdy items of which the following is fairly typical.

As I was riding by the way
   A woman proffered me a bag,
And forty cattle more, to stay
   And give her belly but a swag.

A pox on the whore, they were but scraps
   That I supposed was single money;
The cattle had lice, or else perhaps
   I had light and took her by the coney.

I had not further rode a mile
   But I met with a market-maid
Who sung, the way for to beguile,
   In these same words, and thus she said:

'I see the bull doth bull the cow;
   And shall I live a maiden still?
I see the boar doth brim the sow;
   And yet there is never a Jack for Jill.'

I had some hope, and to her spoke,
   'Sweetheart, shall I put my flesh in thine?'
'With all my heart, Sir! your nose in my arse,'
   Quoth she, 'for to keep out the wind.'

She rode upon a tired mare,
   And to revenge no time withstood,
I bluntly asked pro to occupy her;
   But first she would know wherefore that was good.

'It will make thee lively,' I did say,
   'Put joy and spirit instead of woe.'
'Then occupy my mare, I pray
   Good Sir, for she can hardly go.'

I milder grew, and would but feel:
  She said she was never felt, but kissed;
I was content, and she said, 'Weel,
  Just kiss my bum and feel my fist.'

I was red and pale with shame and spite
  To be so answered of the drab,
That I swore, and spurred, and away did ride,
  And of my wooing was no blab.

6. Baker's Boy

As this anthology shows, poems about the astonishing sexual practices of tradesmen have been current for centuries. In the A-text the horrific consequences of the boy's sexual initiation are spelled out in detail; in the B-text the same effect is obtained by the suggestive clapping sounds in which the audience are expected to participate.

A

Oh the Baker's boy to the Chandler's went
Some candles for to buy,
And when he got to the Chandler's shop
No one did he espy;
  And just as he was leaving the store
  And thinking that all were dead,
  He thought he heard a rub-a-dub-dub
  Right above his head. (*bis.*)

Now the Baker's boy was cunning and wise
And he crept up the stairs,
He crept up on them so silently
He caught them unawares;
  And what should he see but the Chandler's boy
  Between his Mistress's thighs,
  And they were having a rub-a-dub-dub
  Right before his eyes.

And when they saw the Baker's boy
They both were filled with dread,
The Chandler's wife she turned to him,
And this is what she said:
  'Oh Baker's boy if you'll be true,
  If you'll be true and kind,
  Then you shall have your rub-a-dub-dub
  Whenever you feel inclined.'

Now the Baker's boy was filled with joy
At the prospect of such fun,
And he got through the Chandler's wife

When the Chandler's boy had done;
    And when he was on his shorter strokes
    He said to the Chandler's wife
    That he would like a rub-a-dub-dub
    Every day of his life.

The very next morning when he awoke,
All over he did quake,
His eyes were red, his back was sore,
All over he did ache;
    And on the third day to his surprise,
    After he'd done the trick,
    The only result of his enterprise
    Were the pimples on his prick.

The Baker's boy to the Doctor's went,
Some treatment to obtain,
But when he got to the surgery
He heard this sad refrain:
    'Oh Baker's boy, Oh Baker's boy,
    You've been such a bloody fool,
    No more shall you have your rub-a-dub-dub
    I'm going to cut off your tool.'

The moral of this story is,
There's thorns beneath the rose,
Enthusiastic amateurs
Are a bloody sight worse than pros
    So if you meet a maiden fair
    And self-control you lack,
    Before you have your rub-a-dub-dub
    Be sure you wear a mac.

B

The Baker's boy to the Chandler's went
Some candles for to buy,
But when he got inside the shop
No one could he espy
    And just as he was about to go
    Thinking that all were dead

He suddenly heard a (*clap, clap, clap*)
Right above his head.

Now the Baker's boy was cunning and wise
And he crept up the stairs,
And so it happened that suddenly
He caught them unawares;
    And there he saw the Chandler's boy
    Between his mistress' thighs,
    And they were having a (*clap, clap, clap*)
    Right before his eyes.

Now when she saw the Baker's boy
Then she was filled with dread,
She went up to the Baker's boy
And this is what she said:
    'If you will true my secret keep
    Be honest with me and kind,
    You too can have a (*clap, clap, clap*)
    Whenever you feel inclined.'

Oh, the Baker's boy was filled with joy
At the prospect of such fun;
He took one leap at the Chandler's wife,
And the Chandler's wife was done;
    The Baker's boy enjoyed the fun
    He had with the Chandler's wife,
    And he vowed he'd have a (*clap, clap, clap*)
    Every day of his life.

There's a moral to this tale
And this is how it goes,
Though that you'll pay much notice to it
I really don't suppose;
    It's, if you have a lady love
    And self-control you lack,
    Each time you have a (*clap, clap, clap*)
    Be careful to use a mac.

7. Ball of Kirriemuir

According to the Scottish novelist James Barke (in ed. Barke and Sydney Goodsir Smith, *Robert Burns: The Merry Muses of Caledonia*, London 1965), this celebrates an actual barn-dance held near Kirriemuir in the 1880s. Because the females either eschewed knickers or wore open-crotch drawers the men scattered rosehip seeds on the floor so that in 'the stour of the dance the small hip seeds lodged around the pudendal hair and set up a pubic and vaginal itch'. To this erotic impulse was added punch fortified with Spanish fly and a short-burning kerosene lamp that soon brought darkness down on the revellers. Legman (p. 172) dismisses this as fanciful, pointing out that the stanza-pattern of the 'Ball' was determined by the third quatrain of the song 'Blyth Will an' Bessie's Wedding' in the c. 1800 *MMC*:

> Tammie Tamson too was there,
>   Maggie Birnie was his dearie,
> He pat it in amang the hair
>   An' puddled there till he was weary.

A text of the 'Ball' was later included in *Forbidden Fruit* (c. 1875), so we can only be sure that the 'Ball' was current in the mid-Victorian period. Since then it has expanded into epic proportions and is certainly the best-known piece of bawdry in Scotland, many variants being available. In the kailyard novels of J. M. Barrie, who was born there, Kirriemuir became Thrums and the little market town thus achieved some pseudonymous respectability. In the oral tradition, though, Kirriemuir will always be synonymous with the greatest of all Scottish orgies. The A-text is of Scottish origin; the B-text transports the orgy to England, Frank Buchman's Oxford Group and all; and C-text shows an element of gentility creeping in.

A

Did ye hear about the Ball, my lads?
The Ball of Kirriemuir?
Some came for the dancing

But they mostly came to whore.
  Sing balls to your partner,
  Arse against the wall;
  If you canna get fucked on a Saturday night
  Ye'll never get fucked at all!

Four-and-twenty virgins
Came down from Inverness
And when the Ball was over
There were four-and-twenty less!
  Sing balls, &c.

The Elders of the Kirk were there
And horrified to see
Four-and-twenty maidenheads
A-hanging on a tree.
  Sing balls, &c.

There was fucking in the farmyard,
Fucking in the ricks,
Ye couldna hear the music
For the swishing of the pricks.
  Sing balls, &c.

There was fucking in the hallway,
There was fucking on the stairs,
Ye couldna see the carpets
For the cunts and curly hairs.
  Sing balls, &c.

MacAndrew the farmer
Was sorely grieving that
An acre of his winter wheat
Was fairly fuckit flat.
  Sing balls, &c.

The Undertaker he was there
All dressed up in a shroud,
Swinging from the chandelier
And pissing on the crowd.
  Sing balls, &c.

Missus MacGinty she was there
And had us all in fits,
Diving off the mantelpiece
And bouncing on her tits.
  Sing balls, &c.

The village postman he was there
And scared to death of pox,
So he was masturbating
Into a letterbox.
  Sing balls, &c.

The bride was in a bedroom
Explaining to the groom
The vagina not the anus
Is the entrance to the womb.
  Sing balls, &c.

The village cripple he was there,
He wasna up to much;
He lined them up against the wall
And fucked them with his crutch.
  Sing balls, &c.

The chimney sweep was also there,
He didna care a hoot;
He blew a fart behind his cart
And filled the hall with soot.
  Sing balls, &c.

The outcome of the whole affair
Was scores of tender cocks,
At least a dozen bastards
And a cross exchange of pox.
  Sing balls, &c.

But when the Ball was over
The opinion was expressed
That though the dancing it was good
The fucking was the best.
  Sing balls, &c.

B

John Brown the Factor
Was very surprised to see
Four-and-twenty maidenheads
Hanging on a tree.
    Singing who did you last night,
    Arse against the wall,
    If you canna' get fucked on a Saturday night
    You willna' get fucked at all.

The King was in his counting house,
Counting out his pelf,
The Knave was in the pantry
Playing with himself.   •
    Singing who did, &c.

The Queen was in the parlour
Explaining to the groom,
The vagina not the anus
Is the entrance to the womb.
    Singing who did, &c.

Their daughter she was there, Sir,
And she was dressed in green,
They say she had the biggest cunt
The world has ever seen.
    Singing who did, &c.

There was fucking in the farmyard,
Fucking in the ricks,
You couldn't hear the roosters
For the swishing of the pricks.
    Singing who did, &c.

There was fucking in the courtyard,
Fucking in the square,
You could not see the cobbles
For the pricks and curly hair.
    Singing who did, &c.

There was fucking in the farmyard,
Fucking in the byre,

The friction of the arseholes
Set the hay on fire.
  Singing who did, &c.

The village idiot he was there,
Sitting by the fire,
A-masturbating quietly
With an indiarubber tyre.
  Singing who did, &c.

The Bishop of Chichester he was there,
To fuck he would not stoop,
He's always been a bugger
Since he joined the Oxford Group.
  Singing who did, &c.

Mrs McNatherty she was there,
And she was having fits,
A-diving off the mantelpiece
And bouncing on her tits.
  Singing who did, &c.

The Doctor he was there, Sir,
With all his bag of tricks
And when the fun was over
He sterilised the pricks.
  Singing who did, &c.

C

Oh, four and twenty merry maids
Gaed a' to Kerriemuir,
But only ane come back agin
When she was feelin' queer
  At the ball, the ball,
  A ball aben the brig,
  Oh, sic a carry on got on
  It was an awfu' rig.

Oh, some was in the cornyards
And others in the sprots,
Ye couldna see the barn

For bottles wantin' corks,
   At the ball, the ball,
   The ball o' Kerriemuir,
   There's a lot o' folks agree too
   It caused an awful stour.

Oh, Geordie had a hump-ed back,
He said it gaed him pain,
When his jacket-tail was lifted up
Oot flew a cock and hen,
   At the ball, the ball,
   He stopped the Corporation,
   And the hen come tickerlin' oot
   That caused a consternation.

Oh, Kirsty Smith was a' dressed up,
She'd on her lip a blister,
When she was kissin' Tinker Jock
She burst it on his whisker
   At the ball, the ball,
   Oh Kirsty couldna smile,
   For the split she had upon her lip
   Felt like half a mile.

Oh, Peter Clark with Sailing Jean
And sair he tried to coax her,
When they danced the Berlin Reel
She slid against his oxter
   At the ball, the ball,
   He got her hame for keeps,
   Oh, but now he rocks the cradle
   And feed the nowp wi' neeps.

Oh, the minister's daughter she was there,
Oh, she was first of a'
She drink sae muckle whisky
That she couldnae stand ava
   At the ball, the ball,
   To come to the Muir so sweet,
   Oh, but when the ball was at its height
   There's few them left their feet.

Oh, the aul' wife she comes wrigglin' ben
Upon the oxter's staff,
She said she'd dance the Heilan' Fling
And managed wi' a chaff,
    At the ball, the ball,
    She houched and danced and swat,
    Till the beads o' perforation
    Would have faltered Willie's hairt.

Noo but Jimmy on his stum'er leg
Flew off upon his castor
He tried to race wi' Hell's Mare
And on the brae he passed her,
    At the ball, the ball,
    The ball o' Kerriemuir,
    I hope you like that version,
    The other is owre queer.

8. Barnacle Balls the Sailor

The ruthlessly insistent hero of this nautical piece also goes
under the name of 'Bollocky Bill' and 'Barnacle Bill': this
version combines the two. Whatever the sobriquet his inten-
tions are always strictly dishonourable and he has been
knocking on the door for almost a century. Legman (p. 201)
regards it as a descendant of the song 'Wha is that at my
Bower Door' in the c. 1800 *MMC*.

'Who's that knocking on my door?
Who's that knocking on my door?
Who's that knocking on my door?'
Said the fair young maiden.
 'It's me and my crew: we've come for a screw!'
 Said Barnacle Balls the sailor.
 'It's me and my crew: we've come for a screw!'
 Said Barnacle Balls the sailor.

'You may stand upon the mat,
You may stand upon the mat,
You may stand upon the mat'
Said the fair young maiden.
 'To hell with that: you can't fuck a mat!'
 Said Barnacle Balls the sailor.
 'To hell with that: you can't fuck a mat!'
 Said Barnacle Balls the sailor.

'Will you take me to the dance?
Will you take me to the dance?
Will you take me to the dance?'
Said the fair young maiden.
 'To hell with the dance and down with your pants!'
 Said Barnacle Balls the sailor.
 'To hell with the dance and down with your pants!'
 Said Barnacle Balls the sailor.

'What if we should have a child?
What if we should have a child?
What if we should have a child?'

Said the fair young maiden.
  'We'll kill the bugger and fuck for another!'
  Said Barnacle Balls the sailor.
  'We'll kill the bugger and fuck for another!'
  Said Barnacle Balls the sailor.

'If my parents should come home . . .?
If my parents should come home . . .?
If my parents should come home . . .?'
Said the fair young maiden.
  'We'll kill your paw and fuck your maw!'
  Said Barnacle Balls the sailor.
  'We'll kill your paw and fuck your maw!'
  Said Barnacle Balls the sailor.

9. Bastard King of England

Written history relies on meticulous research, popular oral history on malicious gossip. This apocryphal tale of right royal penile rivalry reduces international affairs of state to the status of an absurd affair. As the poem has a strong Gilbertian influence (cf. 'There lived a king, as I've been told', *The Gondoliers*, 11) it is probably a product of the late 1880s. It has been erroneously attributed to Kipling who, so the story goes, was denied the Poet Laureateship on account of it.

The minstrels sing of an English king
Of many long years ago;
He ruled the land with an iron hand
But his mind was weak and low.
He loved to hunt the royal stag
That roamed in the royal wood;
But better by far he loved to sit
And pound the royal pud.
His only undergarment
Was a dirty yellow shirt
With which he tried to hide his hide
But he couldn't hide the dirt.
   He was lousy and dirty and covered in fleas,
   The hair on his balls hung down to his knees,
   God bless the bastard king of England.

Now the Queen of Spain was an amorous dame,
A lascivious wench was she;
She loved to fool with the royal tool
So far across the sea.
So she sent a royal message
With a royal messenger
To invite the King of England
To spend the night with her.
   He was lousy, &c.

King Philip of France he heard of this
And he summoned his royal court;

He said, 'she loves my rival more
Because my tool is short'.
So he sent the Duke of Suffering Sap
To give the queen a dose of clap
To pass it on to the bastard
King of England.
  He was lousy, &c.

When the King of England heard of this
Within the royal hall
He up and swore by the royal whore
He'd have the Frenchman's balls;
He offered half the royal perch
And a piece of Queen Hortense
To any British subject
Who'd outdo the King of France.
  He was lousy, &c.

Now the noble Duke of Middlesex
Betook himself to France;
He swore he was a fairy
So the King let drop his pants.
On Philip's dong he slipped a thong,
Jumped on his horse and galloped along,
Dragging the Frenchman
Back to Merrie England.
  He was lousy, &c.

When they returned to London Town,
Within fair England's shore,
Because of the ride King Philip's pride
Was stretched a yard or more;
And all the whores in silken drawers
Came down to London Town,
And shouted round the battlements
'To hell with the British crown!'
So Philip alone usurped the throne,
His sceptre was the royal bone
With which he beat the bastard
King of England.
  He was lousy, &c.

10. Black Thing

Putting outrageously amorous expressions into the mouth of a female narrator is a favourite device of bawdy poets who thereby hope to gain an added piquancy. The opening quatrain, pastoral in tone, is an ironic introduction to the anti-pastoral sentiments that follow in this eighteenth-century broadside.

Ye nymphs and ye swains that trip over the plains
Come listen a while to my innocent tale,
And hear me with pity while I do sing,
It's no less than the loss of my little black thing.

As I sat at cards with a friend t'other day
To pass some dull hours and drive care away
Young Colin as brisk as a bird in the spring
He wanted to play with my little black thing.

On me his sly looks were constantly bent
To gaze on my beauty it was his intent,
His looks towards me he did frequently fling
While he gently handled my little black thing.

I dreamt of no hurt but thought him quite blunt,
And gave him the pleasure to play with my cunt,
Then got up his pintle quite stiff for a fling,
And ran it slap into my little black thing.

Ten thousand soft whispers he forced in my ear,
I bid him be gone but he still would not hear,
I had no power left from him to spring,
He got so fast hold of my little black thing.

I squeaked and I squealed and bid him let go,
He smiled in my face and answered me no,
A crown in my lap he did instantly fling
To let him enjoy my little black thing.

Then a full pintle he put in my hand,
I wanted no coaxing to make it stand,
I measured it round with a nine-inch string
And found it just fit for my little black thing.

Then I got on the ground and lay on my back,
He drew his pintle and balls my cunt in a crack;
My legs round his body I fixed as a spring
And dragged out the brains with my little black thing.

11. Blind Nell

The fate of Dickens's Little Nell – in *The Old Curiosity Shop* (1841) – had a lachrymose effect on the author and his adoring public. No tears have been shed over this little Nell yet there is a genuinely poignant, if hard-bitten, quality to this poem which has remained in the oral tradition since its appearance in the first quarter of this century.

There's a blind girl lives down our street,
Her name is little Nell.
Can she see the stars above?
Can she fucking hell.

There's a tailor lives down our street,
He works aboard a lugger,
He isn't fit to shovel shit
The dirty lousy bugger.

One night he slept beside our Nell,
He knew it wasn't lawful.
His breath smelt like a sewage farm,
His feet were fucking awful.

Now he's sailed across the seas,
She sends him flowers and parcels;
She thinks he will return to her,
Will he fucking arseholes.

12. Blow the Candle Out

There is a version of this – under the title 'The London Prentice' – in *Pills* so the song has been popular since the seventeenth century, mainly because of its lyrical texture and easy eroticism. The A-text emphasises the warm passion of the couple; the B-text transforms the song into a moralistic tale of betrayal.

A

'Twas a young apprentice boy
   Came courting his dear,
The moon was shining bright
   And the stars were twinkling clear;
He went to his love's window
   To ease her of her pain:
His darling rose and let him in
   Then went to bed again.

It's early next morning
   Before the break of day,
The laddie rose, put on his clothes,
   Aa for to go away;
But when that he was going away
   His love to him called out
'Come, take me in your arms, love,
   And blow the candle out.

My father and my mother,
   They taunt me very sore
For keeping o' your company, love,
   But I will keep it more;
For aa the taunts that they can gie
   They'll never change my heart,
So, come here my dear, and I'll meet you here,
   Let the night be ever so dark.'

'Your father and your mother
   In yonder room do lie,
Embracing one another,
   And so may you and I;

Embracing one another
   Without a fear or doubt,
So, take me in your arms love,
   And blow the candle out.

My bosom is on fire, love,
   The more I gaze on thee,
And as I wander lower
   I am no longer free;
And while I gaze your rosy-lips
   Do sweetly seem to pout,
So hasten to my arms, love,
   And blow the candle out.'

B

There was a young apprentice who went to meet his dear.
The moon was shinin' brightly and the stars were viewin'
   clear.
He went to his love's window and he called her by her name,
Then soon she rose and let him in, went back to bed again.

Sayin', 'Willie, dearest Willie, tonight will be your doom.
Strip off into your nightshirt and bear one night within.
The streets they are too lonely for you to walk about,
So come roll me in your arms, love, and we'll blow the
   candle out.

My father and my mother, next bedroom they do lie,
Kissing and embracing, and why not you and I?
Kissing and embracing without a fear or doubt,
So come roll me in your arms, love, and we'll blow the
   candle out.

It was six months and after six, six months ago today,
He wrote to me a letter saying he was far away;
He wrote to me a letter without a fear or doubt,
And he never said when he'd come back to blow the candle out.

Come all you gallant highway girls pay heed to what I say,
Never court a young man that ploughs the angry sea;
For some day or another when walking out about
He will do to you as he done to me when he blew the candle
   out.'

13. Bold English Navvy

This story of the navvy who died (in the sexual sense) with his boots on originated early in the nineteenth century.

Oh, I'm a bold English navvy that fought on the line,
The first place I met was Newcastle-on-Tyne,
I been tired, sick and weary from working all day,
To a cot down by the hillside I'm making my way.

Oh, I first had me supper and then had a shave.
For courtin' this fair maid I highly prepared.
Th'old stars in the sky as the moon it shone down,
And I hit for the road with my navvy boots on.

I knocked at my love's window – my knock she did know,
And out of her slumber she woken so slow.
I knocked there again and she said, 'Is that John?'
And I quickly replied, 'With my navvy boots on.'

Oh, she opened the window and then let me in.
'Twas into her bedroom she landed me then.
Th'old night it being cold and the blankets rolled on,
And I slept there all night with my navvy boots on.

Oh then, early next morning at the dawn of the day,
Said I to me true love: 'It's time to go away.'
'Sleep down, sleep down, you know you've done wrong
For to sleep here all night with your navvy boots on.'

Oh, he bent down his head with a laugh and a smile,
Saying, 'What could I do, love, in that length of time?
And I know if I done it, I done it in fun,
And I'll do it again with my navvy boots on.'

Oh then, six months being over and seven at the least,
When this pretty fair maid got stout round the waist.
For eight months being over, when nine comes along,
And she handed him a young son with his navvy boots on.

'Oh, come all you pretty fair maids take a warning by me,
Don't ever leave a navvy go into your bed.
For when he'll get warm and think upon yon,
Sure, he'll jump on your bones with his navvy boots on.'

14. Bonnie Wee Lassie Who Never Said No

A nineteenth-century song of sexual betrayal about a positively naïve country lass.

I come to a cross and I met a wee lass,
Says I, 'My wee lassie are you willing to go?'
'Take share of a gill,' she said, 'Sir, I will,
For I'm the wee lassie that never said no.'

It's into an alehouse we merrily did go,
And we never did rise till the cock it did crow;
And it's glass after glass we merrily did toast
To the bonnie wee lassie who never said no.

The landlady opened the door and come in with a smile;
She lifted a chair with freedom and air:
'Here's health to the lass who can jig it in style.'

'O bring us some liquor,' the lassie she cried,
'To cheer up his spirits, I doubt they are low.
For it's not what you do, bring a bottle or two
To the bonnie wee lassie who never said no.'

The drinks she took in being the best of the gin;
Me being myself and sober to be,
For it's glass after glass so merry did toast
Till the lass and the landlady found themsel' fu'.

'Look into my pocket,' the lassie she said,
'There are two and six to pay for your bed;
And for laying me down, you owe me a crown,
Look into my pocket,' the lassie she said.

I put my hand in her pocket and five pound I took,
Says I to mysel', 'I will bundle and go.'
And I bade her good bye, but she made no reply,
This bonnie wee lassie who never said no.

So I rambled awa' by the brimbles o' Clee,
And four or five comrades I chanced for to meet,
I told what I done and laughed at the fun,
But I scarcely could tell them what I had been through.

15. Bonny Kate

This dialogue from the post-Restoration drollery *The New Academy* (1669) offers a rare instance of female reluctance.

'Bonny Kate, kenny Kate, lay thy leg o'er me.
Thou be'st a bonny lass, fain would I mow thee.
Fain would I mow thee, an' thou wouldst let me.
Bonny Kate, kenny Kate, do not forget me.'

'Out away, Johnny lad, I'se am a virgin.
There is no hope, for to get pergin.
For to get pergin I dare not let thee.
Out away, Johnny lad, I'se mun forget thee.'

'Thou be'st young, so is I, let us be doing.
There is no better thing than to be mowing,
Than to be mowing, an' thou wouldst let me.
Bonny Kate, kenny Kate, do not forget me.'

'Why dost thou whimper, thou know'st my mind, Jo.
Would mother suffer me, I would be kind, Jo.
I would be kind, Jo, an' she would let me.
Bonny lad, Johnny lad, I'se ne'er forget thee.'

16. Botany Bay

One of the songs popular with the Beggar's Benison club (see headnote to No. 2). Botany Bay was discovered by Captain Cook in 1770 and so named because of the profusion of plants. In 1787 it was chosen as the site for a penal colony and its association with beauty and wrongdoing quickly acquired bawdy overtones.

Britannia, fair garden of this favoured land,
To a scheme gave her sanction, by Ministry planned,
For transporting her sons who from honour did stray,
To a sweet spot terrestrial, termed Botany Bay.
  Toll de roll, de roll, toll de roll.

Now this Bay, by dunderheads, we've sagely been told,
Was unknown to the famed navigators of old;
But this we deny in terms homely and blunt,
For Botany Bay all through Fife is called cunt.
  Toll, &c.

Our ancestor, Adam, 'tis past any doubt,
Was the famous Columbus that found the spot out;
He braved every billow, rock, quicksand, and shore,
To steer through the passage none e'er steered before.
  Toll, &c.

Kind Nature, ere Adam had pushed off to sea,
Bade him be of good cheer – for his pilot she'd be;
Then his cables he slipped and stood straight for the Bay,
But was stopped on the passage about the midway.
  Toll, &c.

'Avast,' Adam cried, 'I'm dismasted I doubt,
If I don't take the head of my vessel about.'
'Take courage,' cried Nature, 'and leave it to me,
For 'tis only the line that divides the Red Sea.'
  Toll, &c.

Though shook by the stroke, Adam's mast stood upright,
His ballast was steady, his tackling quite right;

Then a breeze springing up, down the red straits he run,
And o'erjoyed with his voyage, he fired off a great gun.
    Toll, &c.

High from the mast-head, by the help of one eye,
The heart of the Bay did old Adam espy;
And alarmed at some noise, to him Nature did say,
That it was the Trade Wind, which blows always one way.
    Toll, &c.

So transported was Adam in Botany Bay,
He Dame Nature implored to spend there night and day;
And curious, he tried the Bay's bottom to sound,
But his line was too short by a yard from the ground.
    Toll, &c.

The time being out, Nature's sentence had passed,
Adam humbly a favour of her bounty asked,
That when stocked with provisions and everything sound,
To Botany Bay he again might be bound.
    Toll, &c.

Nature granted the boon both to him and his race,
And said – 'oft I'll transport you to that charming place,
But never,' cried she, 'as you honour my word,
Set sail with disease or with famine aboard.'
    Toll, &c.

Then this Botany Bay, or whate'er be the name,
We have proved is the spot whence the whole of us came,
May we there be transported, like Adam our sire,
And never return 'fore the time shall expire.
    Toll, &c.

17. Bride's Letter

Because it is such a sustained performance this poem has been attributed, wrongly, to Byron. I would guess, from the strained mock-Augustan diction ('Bright Phoebus', &c), that it had a late Victorian genesis since when it has been frequently circulated in manuscript and typescript.

Dear Belle,
      When we parted you asked me to write
And inform you of all that occurred on the night
When Frank and your Emma were joined hand-in-hand
And allowed to perform all that love can command.
But what language can tell us, the wise man said,
All of the wonderful ways of a man with a maid?
Rest assured they can only be properly known
From a lecture in bed by a swain of your own.
Ne'ertheless I will tell you as well as I can
Of all that I learned of the secrets of man.
When the marriage was over our carriage-and-four,
Well appointed and handsome, drove up to the door.
We started for Dover exactly at noon
To spend, as the phrase is, a snug honeymoon.
Bright Phoebus shone o'er us the whole of the way,
The Captain was amorous, ardent, and gay;
So much so indeed that, although in the carriage,
He began to indulge in the freedom of marriage.
He ventured so far that I felt in a fright
For fear the wild rogue would have ravished me quite.
When we reached our hotel we found all things prepared,
The apartments were handsome, well furnished and aired.
The repast that they served was so stylish and neat
That it seemed quite a sin not to fall to and eat.
But the repast we expected a little while hence
So engrossed every thought and extinguished each sense
That all other desires seemed deadened and gone
And our appetites all became centred in one.
Frank praised the champagne, I thought it delicious,
He declared it enough to make Vesta propitious
And indeed he was right for, between you and me,

36

I never before in my life felt so free.
Now attend and I'll draw the curtain aside
And disclose all the sports of the bridegroom and bride,
Dealing at length with that process bewitching
By which girls are cured of a troublesome itching
And men – though impetuous, hasty and rude –
At length by a woman are tamed and subdued.
You remember how often we tried to discover
All the joys to be found in the arms of a lover
And now this approached I felt all of a pucker
And thought that my breasts would have burst from their
    tucker.
Frank saw my condition and tenderly said,
'You are tired darling Emma, so pray go to bed;
Late hours are the bane and destruction of numbers
So make haste and I'll soon come and watch o'er your
    slumbers.'
What a sly wicked rogue! but I knew what he meant
So, covered with blushes, obliged him and went.
I was scarcely undressed and prepared for my doom
When I heard the dear fellow glide into the room
And as silent I lay between wonder and dread
He threw off his clothes and leaped into bed.
In a moment I found myself clasped in his arms
And immediately lost all my groundless alarms
For he soothed me so fondly and gave me such kisses
As warmed my young heart for more exquisite blisses,
Whilst his bold daring hand in pursuit of its game
Pressed my bosom and wandered all over my frame
And most frequently trespassed, conceive my distress,
Where – my pen cannot write – but I'm sure you can guess.
In tears I implored of him not to be rude
But he sealed up my mouth and his rambles pursued
Declaring 'If men might not do as they wished
This world in a short time would cease to exist.'
This was all very well, but he bade me reflect
That our parents, good souls so refined and select,
Had done the same thing and indeed it was clear
That if they had not we should not have been here.
Moreover he stated, that very same day,
I had promised in church to love and *obey*
And the parson himself in a plain exhortation

37

Had stated that marriage and due copulation
Were sent to check sin and prevent fornication
Hence 'twas plainly quite wrong to preserve such a distance
And keep up such a determined resistance.
My reserve soon was banished and love, unrestrained
By alarms and by coyness, triumphantly reigned.
Then proudly in arms without further delay
Like a lion he eagerly leaped on his prey.
You can scarcely conceive my delightful condition
Whilst his strong awful weapon was gaining admission.
But Oh! what a weapon this wonderful fence is,
Surpassing so far our most exquisite fancies;
So resistless in power and extended in length
That at first when I felt its dimensions and strength
O'ercome with alarm I exclaimed with a cry
'For God's sake forbear or I'm sure I shall die!'
But my tears and my fears alike went unheeded
And, bent on his purpose, the spoiler proceeded
And although he was, as I thought, like a giant
Dame Nature has made us young maidens so pliant
That – expanded – I yielded to every aggression
Until he had gained the completest possession.
Then I found my dear Belle that the saying is true
That a man and his wife are but one and not two,
For union so close all description surpasses
And can scarce be conceived by you innocent lasses.
The conflict now raging was ravishing quite,
My pain became pleasure, my tremor – delight.
The great engine of bliss in perpetual motion
Played its part with such skill and active devotion
That as each eager thrust was successively given
I felt quite exhausted and wafted to heaven.
Round his vigorous frame like a tendril I twined
While our legs in lascivious alliance combined
And we revelled in joy till our transports at last
Reached the climax of Hymen's delightful repast
When by rapt'rous full tide o'erwhelmed and oppressed
With a strong closing effort he lay on my breast.
For some moments entranced dissolving we lay
Whilst the fountains of bliss were briskly at play
And – thrilled through by Venus – an o'erpowering sensation,
He gave the warm pledge to a new generation.

Now although the first transports of passion were spent
My hero on further achievements was bent
For he still kept possession with power unsubdued
And, embracing me closely, his pastime pursued.
Delighted I felt the keen impulse again
And repaid with fresh ardour the feats of my swain
Who – more temperate now – played his amorous part
And repressed the wild force of his soul's erect dart.
Now panting with pleasure, my breath nearly gone,
I courted swift action and whispered 'Go on';
All attention the summons he promptly obeyed
And again the sweet tribute of ecstasy paid.
Thus the first act of wedlock was brought to a close
And – parting – we sank into quiet repose.
But our slumbers were short for, warm fancy possessed
With the scenes that were passed, it were idle to rest.
And my dreams so reflected amours all again
That I started and woke with my blood in a flame.
Thus excited I sought the renewal of bliss
And saluted dear Frank with a warm ardent kiss
Which enthused new desires in his every vein
And soon moved him to love's sweet encounter again.
So he placed in my hand the dear source of my pleasure
And said 'Stroke him gently my darling, my treasure.'
The rogue as I pressed him grew longer and stronger
Till, unable to bear my warm grasp any longer,
He flew to my arms and with one active lilt
Lodged his glorious weapon right up to the hilt
And again we enjoyed our connubial employment
And passed through the night in mutual enjoyment,
Thus alternately sleeping and sporting we lay
Till bright Phoebus had mounted the chariot of day.
Six times we enjoyed our amorous riot
When my hero at length seemed disposed to be quiet
But to tell you the truth had he given me a score
I ardently still would have asked him for more
But, more prudent, he thought it was time to observe
The maxim of keeping a *corps* in reserve
That he would not again appear with such *éclat*
If at first he was made to appear *hors de combat*.
So, grown bold, I extended my warm loving hand
And found my dear playfellow greatly expand

But Frank for a while snugly lay on his back
And said it was my turn to make the attack
So I mounted at once and, as something to brag on,
Enacted the part of St George and the dragon
And accomplished my part with such skill and address
That it quickly was crowned with completest success.
This completed the sports of that wonderful night
And set the last seal on that work of delight
So we rose to perform our respective ablutions
And wash off the stains of our frequent pollutions.
But words after all can but faintly reveal
All the joys that in wedlock you're destined to feel
So lose not a moment my dear Arabella
But fly to the arms of some handsome young fellow.
Make haste and get married as soon as you can
For life's but a blank till enjoyed with a man.
He'll quickly remove any girlish dilemma
And make you as blessed as your happy friend

Emma.

18. Bugger's Alphabet

When the bawdy muse ran out of creative steam it was reduced to mechanical exercises like acrostics and alphabetical verse. This adult alphabet is of twentieth-century origin; the A-text has a certain charm, the B-text a certain desperation, and uses a chorus that dates to *c*. 1810.

A

A is the Artfulness in the words he uses
B is the Blush as she gently refuses
C is the Creep of his hand on her legs
D is the *Don't* she tearfully begs
E is the Excitement his hand getting higher
F is the Feeling of intense desire
G is the Gasp as her garter he touches
H is how Helpless she feels in his clutches
I is the Itching that makes her feel hot
J is the Jump as he reaches the spot
K is the Kiss with which she rewards him
L is the Love she now feels towards him
M is the Movement they make towards bed
N is the Neat way she opens her legs
O is the Opening that's now revealed
P is the Penis already peeled
Q is the Queer way she feels when it's in
R is the Rapture when sweet pains begin
S is the Stroke getting longer and longer
T is the Throb getting stronger and stronger
U is the Unction that now freely flows
V is the Vim he puts in his blows
W is the Wish for it over again
X is the Extent of both pleasure and pain
Y is the Yearning that makes her heart throb
Z is the Zambok he puts on his knob.

B

A is the arsehole all covered in hair
    Hey-ho says Roley!

And B is the bugger who wished he was there
With a roly-poly huff'em and stuff'em
Hey-ho says Anthony Roley!

C is the cunt all covered in piss
Hey-ho says Roley!
And D is the drunkard who gave it a kiss
With a roly-poly, &c.

E is the eunuch with only one ball
Hey-ho says Roley!
And F the poor fucker with no balls at all
With a roly-poly, &c.

G is for goitre, gonorrhea and gout
Hey-ho says Roley!
And H is the harlot who spreads them about
With a roly-poly, &c.

I is for incest, indecent and itch
Hey-ho says Roley!
And J is the jerk of a dog on a bitch
With a roly-poly, &c.

K is the king who shat on the floor
Hey-ho says Roley!
And L is the lousy and licentious whore
With a roly-poly, &c.

M is the maiden all fucked and forlorn
Hey-ho says Roley!
And N is the noble who died on the horn
With a roly-poly, &c.

O is the orifice already revealed
Hey-ho says Roley!
And P is the penis with foreskin well peeled
With a roly-poly, &c.

Q is the quaker who shat in his hat
Hey-ho says Roley!
And R is the rector who buggered his cat
With a roly-poly, &c.

S is the shithouse all full to the brim
Hey-ho says Roley!
And T are the turds that are floating therein
With a roly-poly, &c.

U is the usher of a young maiden's school
Hey-ho says Roley!
And V is the virgin who played with his tool
With a roly-poly, &c.

W is the whore who thought fucking a farce
Hey-ho says Roley!
And X, Y and Z you can stuff up your arse!
With a roly-poly, &c.

19. Butcher

From *The Rattle* (1776): notable for its excruciating puns.

A lusty young butcher near Leadenhall dwelt,
Who never the force of Love's cleaver had felt,
That terrible weapon which always excites,
Such sorrow and joy in the heart where it lights.
   Derry down.

Long time he had boldly defied Cupid's quiver,
Resolving as yet to remain a free liver.
The god grew enraged, and at length gained the battle,
And slaughtered poor Pluck just as he slaughtered cattle.
   Derry down.

It happened one day as he stood at his shambles,
Brisk Dolly, the cook-maid, the sweetest of damsels,
To market for dinner came tripping close by,
At whom the young butcher soon cast a sheep's eye.
   Derry down.

At sight of her beauties what mortal could cool?
Her skin it is said was as soft as lamb's wool;
Her black roguish eyes shone as bright as his steel,
And her nice even teeth were as white as young veal.
   Derry down.

Like other young lovers, he sighed, lied, and swore,
And gazing with rapture her charms he ran o'er.
Then down on his marrow-bones begged for relief,
For ah! he was dying to be in her beef.
   Derry down.

But she had a heart was more hard than his block,
Her virtue he found was as firm as a rock,
She told him, unless he would make her his wife,
He ne'er should be suffered to stick in his knife.
   Derry down.

The heat of his passion his looks did betray,
The flame burned so fierce, he could no longer stay,
To the church they both went, and let it suffice
Old Domine skewered them up in a trice.
  Derry down.

And now, Master Pluck, mind the council here hinted,
All women in love never like to be stinted,
Take care that her mag with raw meat is well fed,
Lest the horns of an ox should adorn your calf's head.
  Derry down.

20. Camel

This beast was probably born during World War One and
has refused to die the death ever since, even acquiring in the
E-text erudite additions complete with an allusion to 'Haldane
and Huxley and Joad'.

A

The urge of the camel for pleasure
Is greater than anyone thinks,
It spends many moments of pleasure
In a hole at the back of the Sphinx.

Now sometimes this useful depression
Is filled with the sands of the Nile
Which accounts for the camel's expression
And the Sphinx's inscrutable smile.

B

The amorous urge of the camel
Is not what the traveller thinks,
For the camel, whose sex life is morbid,
Has immoral designs on the Sphinx.

But the Sphinx's enormous hindquarters
Are deep in the sands of the Nile;
Hence the camel's disgruntled demeanour,
And the Sphinx's inscrutable smile.

C

The sexual desires of the camel
Are greater than anyone thinks;
At the height of the mating season
He tried to bugger the Sphinx.

But the Sphinx's anular passage
Was blocked by the sands of the Nile

Which accounts for the hump on the camel's back
And the Sphinx's inscrutable smile.

D

The sexual life of a camel
Is stranger than anyone thinks;
One night in the sands of the desert
It attempted to bugger the Sphinx,
But the Sphinx's anal channel
Was blocked by the sands of the Nile
Which accounts for the hump on the camel
And the Sphinx's inscrutable smile!

E

The sexual desires of the camel
Are greater than most people think;
At the height of its sexual season
It must go and try bugger the Sphinx.
But the anal canal of that creature
Is blocked by the sands of the Nile
Which accounts for the hump of the camel
And the Sphinx's inscrutable smile.

Now recent exhaustive researches
By Haldane and Huxley and Joad
Have shown that the camel will bugger
Any beast from a whale to a toad
Excepting the African hedgehog
Which Haldane and Huxley have shown
To possess an immunity factor
Which is found in this species alone.

21. Cats on the Rooftops

This was sung, to the tune of 'Do ye ken John Peel', by British troops during World War One as a diverting exercise in *Schadenfreude*.

Cats on the rooftops, cats on the tiles,
Cats with syphilis, cats with piles,
Cats with their arseholes wreathed in smiles!
All revelling in the joys of copulation!

Dogs on the seashore, dogs on the rocks,
Dogs with gonorrhea, dogs with pox,
Dogs with bloody great festering cocks,
All revelling in the joys of copulation!

Sheep in the sheepfold, sheep in lamb,
Sheep in agony, sheep in a jam,
Sheep being fucked by a bloody great ram,
All revelling in the joys of copulation!

The bull rhinoceros, so it seems,
Seldom has to have wet dreams,
But when he does, he comes in streams,
And just revels in the joys of copulation!

The donkey is a funny bloke,
Seldom seems to have a poke,
But when he does he lets it soak
And just revels in the joys of copulation!

Bulls in the paddock, bulls in the corn,
Bulls with the balls' itch, bulls with the horn,
Bulls with their cocks all shaved and shorn
All revelling in the joys of copulation!

Old Brer Terrapin in his shell
Can't get at it very well,
But when he does – Coo! Fucking hell!
He just revels in the joys of copulation!

When you wake up in the morning and you're feeling grand,
And you've such a funny feeling in your seminary gland,
And you haven't got a woman – what's the matter with your
      hand
As you revel in the joys of copulation?

When you wake up in the morning and you're full of joy
And your wife won't let you, and your daughter's coy,
Stick your prick up the arsehole of your second eldest boy
And just revel in the joys of copulation.

22. Charlotte

From the first quarter of the twentieth century, this is a tribute to one of the great whores of bawdry.

A

It was down in old Texas
Where the bullturd lies thick,
I was riding along with my hand on my prick, ·
'Twas there that I met her the girl I adore,
Charlotte the harlot, the cowpunchers' whore.
  Yip I yay, yip I yay,
  Yip I yay, yip I yay,
  Charlotte the harlot, the cowpunchers' whore.

She's lousy, she's frowsy,
She works on the street,
Whenever you meet her she's always on heat.
You can frig her for fourpence no less and no more,
Charlotte the harlot, the cowpunchers' whore.
  Yip I yay, &c.

I've fucked her in darkness,
I've fucked her in light,
And once for a lark fifteen times in one night.
And each time I fucked her I slipped her a quart,
If you don't call that fucking YOU FUCKING WELL
    OUGHT!
  Yip I yay, &c.

B

It was down in Old Texas
Where the bullturd lies thick,
One hand on my saddle and one on my prick,
And who should I see but the girl I adore,
It was Charlotte the harlot, the cowpuncher's whore.

She'll cost you a tanner
She'll cost you a bob,

But that all depends on the size of your knob;
But no matter how thick, no matter how thin,
Charlotte the harlot will cram them all in.

She's easy, she's greasy,
She's my heart's delight,
And I fucks her by day and I fucks her by night,
And each time I fucks her I gives her a quart,
And if you don't call that fucking you fucking well ought.

23. Christopher Colombo

Christopher Columbus, with the support of the king of Spain, set out from Palos on 3 August 1492 and on 12 October sighted America; in this piece, which has certain affinities with 'The Good Ship Venus' (No. 48), he rounds the sexual horn. A Columbian Exhibition in Chicago, 1892, may have inspired the song; Walter Klinefelter (in *Preface to an Unprintable Opus*, Portland, Maine 1942) convincingly suggests it was modelled on Gilbert's 'In enterprise of martial kind' from *The Gondoliers* (1889, 11).

In Fourteen-Ninety-Two
Down in the Spanish alley
A sailor took his cock in hand
And shouted 'Hot tomalley'.
  He said the world was round-O,
  His balls hung to the ground-O,
  That masturbating fornicating
  Sonofabitch Colombo.

Along did come the Queen of Spain,
Her name was Isabella,
She saw at a glance from the lump in his pants
That he was a fine young fella.
  He said, &c.

'O Isabel,' Colombo said,
While playing with his balls,
'The world is round I see,' said he,
'I see that duty calls.'
  He said, &c.

'Just wait a bit,' said Isabel,
'And don't forget essentials;
For I've a mind to have a grind
And check out your credentials.'
  He said, &c.

She gave her guest no time to rest,
The pace was fairly killing;
With legs apart he gave the tart
An extra special filling.
　　He said, &c.

For forty days and forty nights
He sailed the broad Atlantic;
Colombo and his scurvy crew
For want of a screw were frantic.
　　He said, &c.

They spied a whore upon the shore,
And off went coats and collars;
And by the time the sun had set
She made a thousand dollars.
　　He said, &c.

With lustful shout they ran about
And practised fornication;
And when they sailed they left behind
Ten times the population.
　　He said, &c.

And when his men pulled out again
And reckoned all their score up,
They'd caught a pox from every box
That syphilised all Europe.
　　He said, &c.

24. Cock and Broomstick

This description of a painful sexual initiation dates from World War One.

Cock and broomstick, cunt and pole,
Went to fuck a lady, couldn't find the hole,
Found the hole at last, Sir, under her frock,
Give me all the world, Sir, I couldn't find me cock,
Found me cock at last, Sir, under me hand,
Give me all the world, Sir, I couldn't make it stand,
Made it stand at last, Sir, straight as any pin,
Give me all the world, Sir, I couldn't get it in,
Got it in at last, Sir, wriggled it about,
Give me all the world, Sir, I couldn't get it out,
Got it out at last, Sir, all stiff and sore,
Give me all the world, Sir, I wouldn't fuck no more.

25. Cold

A melancholy lament from World War Two when it circulated in mimeograph.

Cold as the hairs on a polar bear's bum,
Cold as a whore when she knows you have come,
Cold as charity and that's bloody chilly
But not so cold as the balls of our Willy
He's dead, poor sod.
   He's dead, poor bugger;
   He's dead, poor bugger;
   He's dead, he's dead, he's dead.

26. Come Live with Me

A popular parody of Christopher Marlowe's 'Come live with me and be my love', it was collected (as 'The Wooing Rogue') in *Westminster Drolleries* (1875).

Come live with me and be my whore
And we will beg from door to door,
Then under a hedge we'll sit and louse us
Until the beadle come to rouse us
And if they'll give us no relief
Thou shalt turn whore and I'll turn thief.

If thou canst rob then I can steal
And we'll eat roast meat every meal;
Nay, we'll eat white bread every day
And throw our mouldy crusts away
And twice a day we will be drunk
And then at night I'll kiss my punk.

And when we both shall have the pox
We then shall want both shirts and smocks
To shift each other's mangy hide
That is with itch so pockified;
We'll take some clean ones from a hedge
And leave our old ones for an pledge.

27. Come on Lads

Teasing rhymes have been popular since the seventeenth century; this example is from World War One.

Come on lads, gather round, here's to a damned good supper,
When you're out with another man's wife you're a fool if you
    don't
Send your kids to school and teach them every trick
For the only thing for a chorus girl is a man with a damned
    big
P stands for Pudding, R stands for Rice,
C stands for something else, it's naughty but it's nice.
When I go out fishing I sit upon a rock,
I never bait my hook with worms, I always use my
Dainty little finger, so slender and so slim,
I can get all five of them into my girl's
Pockets are so useful, when you are in the stalls,
If you feel a trifle bored you can always play with your
Money in your pocket, that's if you're in luck,
And always spend your last ten bob in having a damned good
Turkish bath and a manicure, that makes you feel so smart,
When you're in a lady's presence never let a
Swear word pass your lips, and please refrain from humming,
Or you'll never know when your best girl will think that you
    are coming.

28. Comin' Thro' the Rye

By substituting 'kiss' for 'fuck' Burns made a socially accept-
able version of this song which was collected in the *c.* 1800
MMC.

Gin a body meet a body
   Comin' throu the rye,
Gin a body fuck a body,
   Need a body cry?
   Comin' throu the rye, my jo,
   An' comin' throu the rye;
   She fand a staun o' staunin' graith   *stand/growth*
   Comin' throu the rye.

Gin a body meet a body
   Comin' throu the glen,
Gin a body fuck a body,
   Need the warld ken?
   Comin', &c.

Gin a body meet a body
   Comin' throu the grain,
Gin a body fuck a body,
   Cunt's a body's ain.
   Comin', &c.

Gin a body meet a body
   By a body's sel,
Whatna body fucks a body,
   Wad a body tell?
   Comin', &c.

Mony a body meets a body
   They darena weel avow;
Mony a body fucks a body,
   Ye wadna think it true.
   Comin', &c.

29. Cooper o' Dundee

From *c.* 1800 *MMC*; Burns styled his 'Whare gat ye that happed meal-bannock' on this bawdy original.

Ye coopers and hoopers attend to my ditty,
    I sing o' a cooper who dwelt in Dundee;
This young man he was baith am'rous and witty,
    He pleas'd the fair maids wi' the blink o' his e'e.

He was nae a cooper, a common tub-hooper,
    The most o' his trade lay in pleasin' the fair;
He hoopt them, he coopt them, he bort them, he plugt them,
    An' a' sent for Sandie when out o' repair.

For a twelvemonth or sae this youth was respected,
    An' he was as bisie, as weel he could be;
But business increased so, that some were neglected,
    Which ruined trade in the town o' Dundee.

A baillie's fair daughter had wanted a coopin',
    An' Sandie was sent for, as oft time was he,
He yerkt her sae hard that she sprung an end-hoopin',
    Which banished poor Sandie frae bonny Dundee.

30. Cruising Round Yarmouth

A song, popular since the nineteenth century, which displays a particularly brilliant use of nautical imagery.

While cruisin' round Yarmouth one day for a spree,
I met a fair damsel, the wind blowing free.
I'm a fast going clipper, my kind sir, said she,
I'm ready for cargo, my hold it is free.
   Singing fal-the-ral-laddy, right-fal-the-ral-day,
   Fal-the-ral laddy, right fal-the-ral day.

I gave her the rope and I took her in tow.
From yardarm to yardarm a-towing we go.
I lift up her hatches, found plenty of room,
And into her cabin I stuck my jibboom.
   Singing, &c.

She took me upstairs and her topsails she lowered,
In a neat little parlour she soon had me moored,
She laid in her foresails, her staysails an' all,
With her lily-white hand on my reef-tackle fall.
   Singing, &c.

I said, 'pretty fair maid, it's time to give o'er,
Betwixt wind and water you've ran me ashore.
My shot locker's empty and powders all spent.
I can't fire a shot for it's choked at the vent.'
   Singing, &c.

Here's luck to the girl with the black curly locks.
Here's luck to the girl who ran Jack on the rocks.
Here's luck to the doctor who eased all his pain;
He squared his mainyards; he's a-cruisin' again.
   Singing, &c.

31. Cuckoo's Nest

Perhaps because of its verbal proximity to cuckold, the cuckoo has long had a sexual significance and its nest is an apt erotic metaphor. The A-text has been popular for more than a century; the B-text begins by appropriating the last stanza of 'Blyth Will an' Bessie's Wedding' from the *c*. 1800 *MMC*.

A

There is a thorn bush in oor kail-yard,
There is a thorn bush in oor kail-yard,
At the back of thorn bush there stands a lad and lass
But they're busy, busy hairin' at the cuckoo's nest.

It is thorned, it is sprinkled, it is compassed all around.
It is thorned, it is sprinkled, and it isn't easy found.
She said 'Young man, you're blundering.' I said it was nae
     true,
But I left her with the makin's o' a young cuckoo.

It's hi the cuckin, ho the cuckin, hi the cuckoo's nest,
It's hi the cuckin, ho the cuckin, hi the cuckoo's nest,
I'll gie onybody a shilling and a bottle o' the best
If they'll rumple up the feathers o' the cuckoo's nest.

B

Twa an' twa made the bed,
Twa an' twa lay doon tegither
Fen the bed began te heat,
The ane lay on aboon the ither.

Some like the lassies that's gey weel dressed,
And some like the lassies that's ticht aboot the waist,
But it's in among the blankets that I like best,
To get a jolly rattle at the cuckoo's nest.

32. Cumnock Psalms

Collected by Burns and included in the *c.* 1800 *MMC*, this is
one of the most basic examples of bawdry – the last stanza
matches D. H. Lawrence's fundamental 'Here tha shits an'
here tha pisses' (*Lady Chatterley's Lover*, Harmondsworth 1960,
p. 232).

As I looked o'er yon castle wa',
  I spied a grey goose and a gled;
They had a fecht between them twa,
  And O, as their twa hurdies gade.
    With a hey ding it in, and a how ding it in,
      And a hey ding it in, it's lang today;
    Tal larietal, tallarietal
      Tal larietal, tal larie tay.

She struck up and he strack down.
  Between them twa they made a mowe,   *fuck*
And ilka fart that the carlin gae,   *old woman*
  It's four o' them wad fill a bowe.   *bowl*
    With a hey, &c.

'Temper your tail, Carlin,' he cried,
  'Temper your tail by Venus' law;'
'Double your dunts,' the dame replied,
  'Wha the deil can hinder the wind to blaw!'
    With a hey, &c.

'For were ye in my saddle set,
  And were ye weel girt in my gear,
If the wind o' my arse blaw you out o' my cunt,
  Ye'll never be reckoned a man o' weir.'
    With a hey, &c.

He placed his Jacob whare she did piss,
  And his ballocks whare the wind did blaw,
And he grippet her fast by the goosset o' the arse
  And he gae her cunt the common law.
    With a hey, &c.

33. Cunning Cobbler

Various nineteenth-century broadsides record the come-uppance of the cobbler; the song is still in oral circulation.

This is just a little story, but the truth I'm going to tell,
It does concern a butcher who in Dover Town did dwell;
Now this butcher was possessed of a beautiful wife,
But the cobbler he loved her as dearly as his life.
  Singing fol-the-riddle-i-do, fol-the-riddle-ay.

Now this butcher went to market for to buy an ox,
And then the little cobbler, sly as any fox,
He put on his Sunday coat and courtin' he did go,
To the jolly butcher's wife because he loved her so.
  Singing, &c.

Now when the little cobbler stepped into the butcher's shop.
The butcher's wife knew what he meant and bade for him to
    stop.
'Oh,' says he, 'me darling, have you got a job for me?'
The butcher's wife so cunning, says, 'I'll go up and see.'
  Singing, &c.

Now she went to the bedroom door and gave the snob a call;
'I have got an easy job if you have brought your awl.
And if you do it workmanlike some cash to you I'll pay.'
'Oh, thank you,' said the cobbler, and began to stitch away.
  Singing, &c.

But as the cobbler was at work a knock come on the door.
The cobbler scrambled out of bed and laid upon the floor.
'Oh,' said she, 'me darling, what will me husband say?'
But then she let the policeman in along with her to play.
  Singing, &c.

But the butcher came from market in the middle of the night,
The policeman scrambled out of bed and soon got out of sight.
The butcher's wife so nimbly locked the bedroom door,
But in her fright she quite forgot the cobbler on the floor.
  Singing, &c.

But the butcher soon found out when he laid down in bed.
'Something here is very hard,' the butcher smiled and said.
She says, 'It is me rolling pin.' The butcher he did laugh:
'How come you for to roll your dough with a policeman's
    staff?'
   Singing, &c.

Now the butcher threw the truncheon on underneath the bed.
There he cracked the piddle pot and hit the cobbler's head.
The cobbler cried out, 'Murder!' Said the butcher, 'Who are
    you?'
'I am the little cobbler that goes mending ladies' shoes.'
   Singing, &c.

'If you are the little cobbler, come along with me,
I'll pay you for your mending before I've done with thee.'
He put him in the bullpen, the bull began to roar,
The butcher laughed to see the bull a-roll him o'er and o'er.
   Singing, &c.

Now early in the morning just as people got about,
The butcher mopped his face with blood, then he turned him
    out.
He pinned a ticket to his back and on it was the news:
'This cobbler to the bedroom goes mending ladies' shoes.'
   Singing, &c.

34. Cunt

There is internal evidence of wishful thinking in this complaint from *The Pearl* (1 July 1879).

Cunt is a greedy, unsatisfied glutton.
All women are ready to yield up their mutton;
Finger them, fuck them, and do as you please
They have such an itching you never can tease;
Thrust in your penis from morning till night,
Still they are ready to come with delight;
Of bollocks and all you could give them galore,
By God! They're so greedy they still cry for more.

Fuck till your penis no longer will stand,
She still your bollocks will tease with her hand;
Rub it, and dandle it over again,
Still she will have it, though writhing with pain;
Let it be long, or let it be thick,
Women are never contented with prick:
And when all their power and vigour are past
With prick in their hand, they will breathe out their last.

35. Derby Ram

In the opinion of Legman (p. 424) the song 'is clearly related to the totemistic ram-dancers of England . . . [who] dressed or disguised in the animal's skin', the function of their mid-winter ritual being to bring fertility in the coming year. Thus the ram has a root in prehistory; this version, with teasing rhymes, is modern.

There was a ram of Derbyshire,
It had two horns of brass;
One grew out of the middle of its head
And the other grew out of its
> *If you don't believe me*
> *And think I'm telling a lie*
> *Just ask the girls of Derbyshire*
> *They'll tell you the same as I.*

When the ram was young, Sir,
It had a peculiar trick
Of jumping over five-barred gates
And landing on its
> *If you don't believe me, &c.*

When the ram was middle-aged
It used to caper round
And all the girls of Derbyshire
Came over to be
> *If you don't believe me, &c.*

When the ram was old, Sir,
They carried it on a truck
And all the girls of Derbyshire
Came down to have a
> *If you don't believe me, &c.*

When the ram was dead, Sir,
They buried it in St Paul's;
It took ten men and a fire brigade
To carry one of its
> *If you don't believe me, &c.*

In the resurrection
The ram it was a 'hoss'
And all the lads of Derbyshire
Came down to have a
  If you don't believe me, &c.

36. Down in the Valley

Preserved orally since the beginning of the century, it has developed from a tender encounter to a tale of retribution.

A

First time I met her I met her in green,
    All in green, all in green,
Best girl I'd ever seen
    Down in the valley where she followed me.

Next time I met her I met her in blue,
    All in blue, all in blue,
Best girl I ever knew
Down in the valley where she followed me.

Next time I met her I met her in brown,
    All in brown, all in brown,
I turned her upside down
Down in the valley where she followed me.

Next time I met her I met her in black,
    All in black, all in black,
I laid her on her back
Down in the valley where she followed me.

Next time I met her I met her in grey,
    All in grey, all in grey,
With her I had my way
Down in the valley where she followed me.

Next time I met her I met her in fawn,
    All in fawn, all in fawn,
Her child had just bin born
Down in the valley where she followed me.

Next time I met her I met her in red,
    All in red, all in red,
I broke her bloody head
Down in the valley where she followed me.

B

The first time I met her
She was all dressed in white,
    All in white, all in white,
She held my hand so tight
Down in the valley where she followed me.

The next time I met her
She was all dressed in brown,
    All in brown, all in brown,
I had her knickers down
Down in the valley where she followed me.

The next time I met her
She was all dressed in puce,
    All in puce, all in puce,
I lost a lot of juice
Down in the valley where she followed me.

The next time I met her
She was all dressed in fawn,
    All in fawn, all in fawn,
One little brat was born
Down in the valley where she followed me.

The next time I met her
She was all dressed in black,
    All in black, all in black,
Boards nailed across the crack
Down in the valley where she followed me.

The next time I met her
She was all dressed in green,
    All in green, all in green,
I went where the nails had been
Down in the valley where she followed me.

C

The first time I met her I met her in white,
The first time I met her I met her in white,
    All in white, all in white,

I kissed her that first night
Down in the valley, the valley so low.

The next time I met her I met her in green,
The next time I met her I met her in green,
   All in green, all in green,
Best tits I've ever seen
Down in the valley, the valley so low.

The next time I met her I met her in brown,
The next time I met her I met her in brown,
   All in brown, all in brown,
I got her knickers down
Down in the valley, the valley so low.

The next time I met her I met her in pink,
The next time I met her I met her in pink,
   All in pink, all in pink,
She made my fingers stink
Down in the valley, the valley so low.

The next time I met her I met her in red,
The next time I met her I met her in red,
   All in red, all in red,
I broke her maidenhead
Down in the valley, the valley so low.

The next time I met her I met her in blue,
The next time I met her I met her in blue,
   All in blue, all in blue,
I fucked her through and through
Down in the valley, the valley so low.

The next time I met her I met her in grey,
The next time I met her I met her in grey,
   All in grey, all in grey,
She's in the family way
Down in the valley, the valley so low.

The last time I met her I met her in check,
The last time I met her I met her in check,

All in check, all in check,
She broke my fucking neck
Down in the valley, the valley so low.

37. Duncan Davidson

Burns based his genteel song of the same name on this item which was collected in the *c.* 1800 *MMC.*

There was a lass, they ca'd her Meg,
    An' she gaed o'er the muir to spin;
She fee'd a lad to lift her leg,
    They ca'd him Duncan Davidson.

Meg had a muff and it was rough,
    Twas black without and red within,
An' Duncan, case he got the cauld,
    He stole his highland pintle in.

Meg had a muff, and it was rough,
    And Duncan strak tway handfu' in;
She clasp'd her heels about his waist,
    'I thank you Duncan! Yerk it in!!!'

Duncan made her hurdies dreep,
    In Highland wrath, then Meg did say;
O gang he east, or gang he west,
    His ba's will no be dry today.

38. Ellibanks

Included in *c.* 1800 *MMC*; a favourite song of Burns's.

Ellibanks and Ellibraes,
    My blessin's ay befa' them,
Tho' I wish I had brunt a' my claes,   *burnt*
    The first time e'er I saw them:
Your succar kisses were sae seet,   *sugar*
    Deil damn me gin I ken, man,
How ye gart me lay my legs aside,   *made*
    And lift my sark mysel, man.   *shift*

There's no a lass in a' the land,
    Can fuck sae weel as I can;
Louse down your breeks, lug out your wand,   *loosen*
    Hae ye nae mind to try, man:
For ye're the lad that wears the breeks,
    And I'm the lass that loes ye;
Deil rive my cunt to candle-wicks,   *tear*
    Gif ever I refuse ye!!!

I'll clasp my arms about your neck,
    As souple as an eel, jo;
I'll cleek my houghs about your arse,   *hook/thighs*
    As I were gaun to speel, jo;   *climb*
I'll cleek my houghs about your arse,
    As I were gaun to speel, jo;
And if Jock thief he should slip out,
    I'll ding him wi' my heel, jo.   *hit*

Green be the broom on Ellibraes,
    And yellow be the gowan!
My wame it fistles ay likes flaes,   *belly/fidgets/flies*
    As I come o'er the knowe, man: *hillock*
There I lay glowran to the moon,   *gazing*
    Your mettle wadna daunton,   *awe*
For hard your hurdies hotch'd aboon, *buttocks jerked above*
    While I below lay panting.

39. Eskimo Nell

With its arresting opening, its consistently clever internal rhymes, and its marvellous terminal pun, the A-text deserves recognition as one of the great modern ballads, while Eskimo Nell herself should be considered with the most heroic of modern heroines. It is the work of a master and it is a tribute to its brilliance that the common reader should have attributed it, quite mistakenly, to Noel Coward, 'the Master'. Because it is so obviously influenced by Robert Service it must have been composed after the appearance of his *Songs of a Sourdough* – which includes 'The Shooting of Dan McGrew' – in 1907. Since then it has become a classic and as such deserves to be preserved in print. The B-text shows how Nell's proportions diminish when her feats are left at the mercy of an unreliable memory.

A

When men grow old and their balls grow cold
And the end of their tool turns blue,
Far from that life of Yukon strife
They'll tell a tale that's true.

So bring me a seat and buy me a drink
And a tale to you I'll tell
Of Deadeye Dick and Mexico Pete
And a whore named Eskimo Nell.

When Mexico Pete and Deadeye Dick
Set out in search of fun
It's Deadeye Dick who wields the prick
And Mexico Pete the gun.

When Deadeye Dick and the greaser runt
Were sore distressed and sad
'Twas mostly cunt that bore the brunt
Though shootings weren't so bad.

When Deadeye Dick and Mexico Pete
Went down to Deadman's Creek

They'd had no luck in the way of a fuck
For well nigh over a week.

Bar a moose or two or a caribou
And a bison cow or so,
But Deadeye Dick was the King of Pricks
And he found such fucking slow.

So Deadeye Dick and Mexico Pete
Set out for the Rio Grande;
Deadeye Dick with swinging prick
And Pete with gun in hand.

And thus they blazed their randy trail
And none their fire withstood
And many a bride who was hubby's pride
Knew pregnant widowhood.

They hit the bank of the Rio Grande
At the height of blazing noon;
To slake their thirst and do their worst
They sought Red Kate's saloon.

And as they strode into the bar
Both prick and gun flashed free:
'According to sex you drunken wrecks
You drinks or fucks with me.'

They knew the fame of our hero's name
From the Horn to Panama
So with little worse than a muttered curse
Those dagos lined the bar.

The women knew his playful ways
Way down on the Rio Grande
So forty whores tore down their drawers
At Deadeye Dick's command.

They saw the fingers of Mexico Pete
Touching his pistol grip;
They didn't waste, in frantic haste
Those whores began to strip.

Deadeye Dick was breathing hard
With noisy snarls and grunts
As forty arses came into view
To say nothing of forty cunts.

Now forty arses and forty cunts
You'll find, if you use your wits
And if you're good at arithmetic,
Signifies eighty tits.

Now eighty tits is a goodly sight
To a man with a mighty stand;
It may be rare in Berkeley Square
But not on the Rio Grande.

Now to test his wind he'd had a grind
The previous Saturday night
And this he'd done to show his fun
And whet his appetite.

His phallic limb was in fighting trim
So he backed and took a run,
He took a jump at the nearest rump
And scored a hole in one.

He bore her to the sandy floor
And fairly fucked her fine,
But though she grinned it put the wind
Up the other thirty-nine.

For when Deadeye Dick performs the trick
There's scarcely time to spare
For with speed and strength on top of length
He fairly singes hair.

Now Deadeye Dick he fucks 'em quick
And had cast the first aside;
He made a dart at the second tart
When the swing doors opened wide.

Then entered in that hall of sin,
Into that house of hell

A lusty maid no whit afraid,
Her name was Eskimo Nell.

Now Deadeye Dick had got his prick
Well into number two
When Eskimo Nell let out a yell
And called to him 'Hi You!'

He gave a flick of his muscular prick
And the whore flew over his head;
He turned about with a snarl and a shout
And his face and his knob were red.

Eskimo Nell she stood it well
As she looked between his eyes;
She glanced with scorn upon his horn
Steaming between his thighs.

She stubbed out the butt of her cigarette
On the end of his gleaming knob
And so utterly beat was Mexico Pete
That he quite forgot his job.

It was Eskimo Nell who was first to speak
In accents clear and cool,
'You cunt-struck shrimp of a Yankee pimp,
Do you call that thing a tool?

And if this here town can't take it down,'
She sneered at the cowering whores,
'Here's a cunt that can do the stunt:
Eskimo Nell, for yours!'

She removed her garments one by one
With an air of conscious pride
Till there she stood in her womanhood
And they saw the Great Divide.

'Tis fair to state 'twas not so great
Though its strength lay well within
And a better word, that's quite often heard,
Would not be cunt but quim.

She laid her down on the table top
Whereon was set a glass;
With a flick of her tits she ground it to bits
Between the cheeks of her arse.

She bent her knees with supple ease
And spread them wide apart,
And with smiling nods to the randy sods
She gave him the cue to start.

Now Deadeye Dick he knew a trick
Or two and he took his time;
For a Miss like this was perfect bliss
So he played in a pantomime.

He flicked his foreskin up and down,
He made his balls inflate
Until they resembled two granite knobs
Upon a garden gate.

He winked his arsehole in and out
And his balls increased in size;
His mighty prick grew twice as thick
And nearly reached his eyes.

He polished it well with alcohol
To get it steaming hot
And, to finish the job, he peppered the knob
With the cayenne pepper pot.

He didn't back and take a run
Or make a flying leap;
He didn't swoop but made a stoop
And a steady forward creep.

With peering eyes he took a sight
Along that fearsome tool;
And the long slow glide as it slide inside
Was calculating – cool.

Now you all have seen the pistons gleam
On the mighty C.P.R.

With the driving force of a thousand horse
So you know what pistons are

Or you think you do if you've yet to view
The power that drives the prick
Or the work that's done on a nonstop run
By a man like Deadeye Dick.

None but a fool would challenge his tool,
No thinking man would doubt;
For his fame increased as the Great High Priest
Of the ceaseless in-and-out.

But Eskimo Nell was an infidel
And equalled a whole harem,
With the strength of ten in her abdomen
And a Rock of Ages' beam.

Amidships she could stand a rush
Like the flush of a water closet,
So she gripped his cock like the Chatwood Lock
Of the National Safe Deposit.

But Deadeye Dick would not come quick –
He meant to conserve his powers;
When in the mind he'd grind and grind
For more than a couple of hours.

She lay a while with a subtle smile
And then her grip grew keener
And with a sigh she sucked him dry
With the ease of a vacuum cleaner.

She did this feat in a way so neat
As to set at grand defiance
The primary cause of the basic laws
That govern all sexual science.

She simply rode that phallic tool
That for years had stood the test,
And accepted rules of the ancient schools
In a second or two went west!

And now my friend we near the end
Of this copulative epic
For the effect on Dick was so sudden and quick
'Twas akin to an anaesthetic.

He slid to the floor and knew no more,
His passion extinct and dead;
He didn't shout as his tool slipped out
Though 'tis said she'd stripped the thread.

Then Mexico Pete he rose to his feet
To avenge his friend's affront
And his tough-nosed colt with a savage jolt
He rammed right up her cunt.

He shoved it hard to the trigger guard
And fired it twice times three
But to his surprise she closed her eyes
And squealed in ecstasy.

As she rose to her feet she looked so sweet
'Bully!' she cried, 'for you,
Though I might have guessed it's about the best
That you poor sods could do.

When next, my friends, you two intend
To sally forth for fun,
Get Deadeye Dick a sugar stick
And buy yourself a bun.

For I'm away to the frozen North
Where pricks are big and strong,
Back to the land of the frozen stand
Where the nights are six months' long.

When you stick it in it's as hard as sin
In a land where spunk is spunk,
Not a trickling stream of lukewarm cream
But a solid frozen chunk.

Back to the land where they understand
What it means to copulate,

Where even the dead lie two in a bed
And the children masturbate.

Back once more to the sins of men,
To the Land of the Midnight Sun;
I go to spend a worthy end
For the North is calling *"Come!"*.'

B

When a man grows old, and his balls grow cold
And the end of his knob turns blue,
And it bends in the middle like a one-string fiddle,
He can tell you a tale or two.

So light my pipe, and fill my glass,
And I a tale will tell
Of Deadeye Dick and Mexico Pete
And a whore called Eskimo Nell.

Now Deadeye Dick and Mexico Pete,
Had been working in Deadman's Creek,
And they'd had no luck in the way of a fuck
For nigh on half a week

Except for a moose or a caribou,
An occasional dead horse or so,
And Deadeye Dick, that King of Pricks,
Found things were fucking slow.

Now when Deadeye Dick and Mexico Pete
Went out for a bit of fun,
It was Deadeye Dick who swung the prick,
And Mexico Pete the gun.

And as they blazed their rocky trail,
No man their path withstood,
And many a bride, who was hubby's pride,
Mourned in pregnant widowhood.

They reached the banks of the Rio Grande
Nigh on a burning noon,

And to slake their thirst and do their worst
They sought Red Jake's saloon.

A score of gamblers thronged the room
And to these says Dick, says he,
'According to your sex, you bloody wrecks,
You drink or you fuck with me.'

Now every man had heard of Dick,
From the Pole to Panama,
So with nothing worse than a muttered curse
Those dagos sought the bar.

And women too had heard of Dick,
Down on the Rio Grande,
And forty whores drew down their drawers
At Deadeye Dick's command.

Now forty whores are a pretty sight
And if you have any wits,
Forty whores and forty drawers
Signifies eighty tits.

Now Dick took a jump at the nearest rump,
And scored a hole in one,
With mighty prick, old Deadeye Dick
Soon settled to the fun.

He bore that whore right to the floor,
And fucked her mighty fine,
The whore she grinned but it fair put the wind
Up the other thirty-nine.

Now Deadeye Dick he fucked them quick,
He cast the first aside,
He made a start on the second tart
When the swingdoors opened wide.

And into that den of vice there stepped,
Into that harlots' hell,
A simple maid, who was unafraid,
And her name was Eskimo Nell.

She cast one glance at the quivering whore,
And she spoke like a maid from school,
'You pallid pimp of a Yankee shrimp,
Do you call that thing a tool?'

And still to Dick, 'You useless prick,
If you really want to screw,
There's still one cunt which'll do the stunt,
It's Eskimo Nell for you.'

Now Eskimo Nell began to strip
Wearing a smile of pride,
Until she stood in her womanhood
And we saw the great divide.

And Eskimo Nell lent over the bar,
Where someone had left a glass,
With a flick of her tits she crushed it to bits
Between the cheeks of her arse.

Now Deadeye Dick, he knew a trick
To warm her gaping slot,
To make it hot he sprinkled the top
With a cayenne pepper-pot.

Now Deadeye Dick he warmed his prick,
And his balls he did inflate,
Till they stood out clear like two granite spheres
Upon a garden gate.

Now Deadeye Dick didn't mean to come,
He meant to preserve his power,
For when he'd a mind he could grind and grind
For many a solid hour.

But Eskimo Nell she cleaned him out
With the ease of a well-trained gleaner,
Without batting an eye she sucked him dry
With the ease of a vacuum cleaner.

Nell felt the flush amidships
Like the flush of a water-closet,

But she gripped his cock, like the Chilward lock
On the National Safe Deposit.

Now Deadeye Dick and Mexico Pete
Have gone from the Rio Grande,
Deadeye Dick with his useless prick
And Pete with his gun in his hand.

And Eskimo Nell has gone back to the Yukon,
The land where spunk is spunk,
Not a dribbling stream of lukewarm cream,
But a solid frozen chunk.

40. Family

A twentieth-century dismissive account of the supposed sexual eccentricities of the aristocracy. Lady Jane was a popular vaginal personification long before Lawrence immortalised her in *Lady Chatterley's Lover* (Harmondsworth 1960, p. 219): 'John Thomas! Dost want *her*? Dost want my lady Jane?'

The family took it much to heart
When Lady Jane became a tart;
But blood is blood and race is race
And so, to save the family's face,
They bought her an exclusive beat
On the shady side of Jermyn Street.

The family loathed it even more
When Marguerite became a whore;
They felt they could not do the same
As they had done for Lady Jane
So bought her an expensive flat
With WELCOME written on the mat.

The gentry came from far and wide
Upon that noble quim to ride;
No balls might nestle 'gainst her charms
Unless they bore a coat of arms!
And so before her son was set
She'd fucked her way right through Debrett!

'Twas even less to the family's fancy
When Lord De Vere became a nancy;
And so in order to protect 'em
They had tattooed around his rectum:
'*Lesser folk must travel steerage,*
This passage is reserved for peerage.'

41. Foggy Foggy Dew

Late eighteenth-century in origin, this exists in dozens of variants. Equally there are dozens of explanations of the enigmatic phrase 'foggy dew' which has been taken to mean virginity. From the evidence of the A-text, the earliest extant copy (c. 1815: John Bell's papers in King's College Library, Newcastle), the 'foggy dew' is a corruption of the bogeyman 'the Bogle bo'; the B-text introduces a tragic note.

A

'When I was in my prenticeship and learning of my trade,
I courted my master's daughter which made my heart right
    glad.
I courted her both summer days and winter nights also,
But I could never her favour win till I hired the Bogle bo.

Day being gone and night coming on, my neighbour he took
    a sheet,
And straight into her room he went just like a wandering
    spirit.
She running up and down, not knowing where to go,
But right into my bed she went for fear of the Bogle bo.

So my true love and me both fell fast asleep,
But ere the morn at fair daylight, sore sore did she weep.
Sore sore did she weep, sore sore did she mourn,
But ere she rose and put on her clothes, the Bogle bo was gone.'

'You've done the thing to me last night, the thing you cannot
    shun
You've taken from me my maidenhead, and I am quite
    undone.
You've taken from me my maidenhead, and brought my body
    low
But, kind sir, if you'll marry me, I will be your jo.'

Now he's married her and taen her hame and it was but his
    part.
She's proved to him a loving wife and joy of all his heart.

He never told her of the joke, nor ne'er intends to do,
But aye when his wife smiles on him, he minds the Bogle bo.

B

Oh, I am a bachelor and I live alone,
And I work in the weaver's trade;
And the only thing that I ever done wrong,
Was courtin' a fair young maid.
I courted her one summer time
And all the winter, too,
And the only thing that I never should have done,
Was to save her from the foggy, foggy dew.

I got that tired of living alone,
I says to her one day,
'I've a nice little crib in my old shack
Where you might safely lay;
You'll be all right in the summer time
And in the winter, too,
And you'll lay right warm and take no harm,
Away from the foggy, foggy dew.'

'I don't think much of this old shack,
And I shall lonely be
With only that poor old Cyprus cat
To keep me company.
There's a cricket singing on the hearth,
And what can that thing do,
If the night turn raw and the fire won't draw,
To save me from the foggy, foggy dew?'

One night she come to my bedside
Time I laid fast asleep,
She puts her head down on my bed
And she starts in to weep;
She yelled and cried, she well near died,
She say, 'What shall I do?'
So I hauled her into bed and I covered up her head
To save her from the foggy, foggy dew.

Says I, 'My dear, lay close to me
And wipe away them tears.'

Then I hauled her shift up over her head
And I wrapped it round her ears.
We was all right in the winter time
And in the summer, too;
And I held her tight that live-long night
To save her from the foggy, foggy dew.

'Now lay you still, you silly young fool,
And don't you feel afraid.
For if you want to work with me
You got to learn your trade.'
I learned her all that summer time
And all the winter, too,
And truth to tell she learned that well;
She saved us from the foggy, foggy dew.

One night I laid there good as gold
And then she say to me:
'I got a pain without my back
Where no pain ought to be.
I was all right in the summer time
And in the winter, too,
But I've took some ill or a kind of a chill
From laying in the foggy, foggy dew.'

One night she start to moan and cry
Says I, 'What's up with you?'
She say, 'I never should've been this way
If that hadn't've been for you.'
I got my boots and trousers on,
I got my neighbour too,
But do what we would, we couldn't do no good,
And she died in the foggy, foggy dew.

So I am a bachelor, I live with my son
And we work in the weavin' trade;
And every time I look in his face I can see
The eyes of that fair young maid;
It reminds me of the summer time,
And of the winter, too,
And the many, many nights she laid in my arms,
To save her from the foggy, foggy dew.

42. Four Old Whores

Legman (p. 414) traces this boasting song back five centuries to its origins in 'A Talk of Ten Wives' – 'the oldest surviving erotic folksong in English' – and points out its similarity to 'Our John's Brak Yestreen' (from *c*. 1800 *MMC*). The number of whores varies from an unholy trinity to this recent quartet.

Four old whores from Winnipeg
Were drinking beer and wine,
One of them said to the other three
'Your hole is smaller than mine.'

The first old whore from Winnipeg said
'Mine is as big as the air;
The birds fly in, the birds fly out,
And never tickle a hair.'

The second old whore from Winnipeg said
'Mine is as big as the moon;
The men jump in, the men jump out,
And don't come out till June.'

The third old whore from Winnipeg said,
'Mine is as big as the sea,
The ships sail in, the ships sail out,
And they never bother me.'

The fourth old whore from Winnipeg said,
'Mine is the biggest of all;
A man went in in the springtime
And didn't come out at all.'

43. Frigging

This eighteenth-century masturbatory fantasy is from a MS (19.3.16) in the National Library of Scotland.

Men when robust and strong are apt to love,
They marry straight that they may easy prove
And all the good that they gain by a wife
Is to be forced to fuck them or have strife.
To duty oft they go without desire
When wives cry out 'O husband you lack fire!'
Some men there are – to purchase sweet repose –
Go out a-fucking and so lose their nose:
None pities them, they're mocked by all that's wise.
And others frig when swelling prick doth rise.
Of these three ways I think the last the best
To give a man all quiet, ease and rest.
The hand doth take what man can freely spare
And yet abstaining gives the hand no care.
If what's most worthy we should still desire
Then men we should, not women, e'er admire.
Since men do fuck the ladies they love most,
I'll fuck myself, from off all court or coast.

44. Frisky Mots of London

This metrical catalogue of awful puns is from the Victorian songbook *The Coal Hole Companion* (*c.* 1844).

If you're inclined to have a treat
Or looking out for lovejoys sweet
Stroll up the Haymarket or Bond Street
   Where nightly there is fun done;
If desire your mind doth tease
And you will pay the usual fees
You very quickly can get ease
   From the frisky mots of London.

The swell, all raging with love's fire,
When he a woman does require,
Selects the girl he doth admire
   Though often he gets undone;
Though he, indeed (the truth I've said)
Is stiff with pride, he need not dread:
He's quickly made to droop his head
   By the frisky mots of London.

The barber is a merry soul
So with the women takes a stroll
And very soon erects his pole
   Resolved to be by none done;
With pleasure at his pole they stare,
His lather-box and all his ware,
His pole and box suit to a hair
   The frisky mots of London.

The jolly tar so full of glee
Admires the tempting open C
And very dearly likes to be
   In a port-hole where there's fun done;
Of treasure he has got a hoard
To spend a deal he can afford
So very soon he goes aboard
   The frisky mots of London.

The fishmonger's a frisky blade
And though he dearly likes a maid
For any flat-fish he's the blade
   And thinks he's not by one done;
So up the quadrant he doth plod,
The girls all follow at his nod,
To give him summat for his cod,
   The frisky mots of London.

The pawnbroker is sure to win,
The blowens he blows out with gin
So in return they take him in
   And vow he is by none done;
When up the spout he stands alone
And this I'm certain you will own:
The pawnbroker's balls are very well known
   To the frisky mots of London.

Old gentleman of sixty-four
With lust and lechery plagued so sore
Resolves to kiss a mot once more
   To prove he is not undone;
No matter what his form or tan
If he's got money please he can,
There's nothing like an old gentleman
   To the frisky mots of London.

So in every rank in every stage
Love and luxury are the rage
But the women can your fire assuage
   They really are by none done;
If you a warm bath do require
Or are stiff with cold (I'm no liar)
You soon may get as hot as fire
   With the frisky mots of London.

45. Fruitful Ground

A seventeenth-century complaint whose classical allusions (to
Medea, whose serpentine hair transformed beholders to stone;
to Nestor, whose longevity was legendary; to Medea, who had
the power to rejuvenate men) suggest a scholarly author.

I am not ill-favoured, halt or lame,
But lusty youth in me is found,
My husband he is much to blame,
To let me lie like fallow ground.
His piercing coulter and his share
Are ready his neighbour's land to till,
But of his own he hath no care.
My fruitful ground lies fallow still.

At night when he comes home to bed
He lies much like a senseless stone,
Transformed like Medusa's head,
For life and courage he hath none.
Nestor that lived three hundred years
May now as much as he fulfil.
His hackney hangs down his head and ears.
My fruitful ground lies fallow still.

I do by him as Medea did cure,
With charms oft to enchant his tool.
I handle it, I dandle it, I stroke it fair,
And all to raise his courage cool,
And yet he lies with rolling eyes.
I use the art of wanton's skill.
No spell nor charms his courage can raise.
My fruitful ground lies fallow still.

In summertime when harvest comes
And every man his corn doth mow,
My husband lies upon his back.
How can he reap that does not sow?

Yet I protest, without all doubt
If he my ground no better till,
Unto the half I'll let it out.
My ground shall not lie fallow still.

46. Fucking Machine

The Victorian obsession with mechanical progress inevitably led to the imaginary device of the A-text (from *The Pearl*, 18 December 1880); during World War One, as the B- and C-texts show, the contraption became uncontrollable.

A

Dear Mary, I promised to write directly to school I returned,
But I think when this letter is finished 'twere better by far it
    were burned;
For a girl has just now returned to us, and bought while in
    town she has been
The last new improvement in dildoes – the new patent
    Fucking Machine.
At night when we go to our bedrooms, we go in for a jolly-
    good spree.
And first I perform upon Fanny and then she performs upon
    me.
It beats the old 'flatcocks' a long way, you know the old game
    that I mean,
O mustn't a man be galoptious if he beats the new Fucking
    Machine?
It beats fingers by far too – a long way, its shape is just like a
    tool,
The girl who owns it's good-natured, she has fucked, I
    believe, the whole school;
She has it herself much too often, and is getting most awfully
    lean,
And her pussy's quite tender with using the patent new
    Fucking Machine.
It gives a delightful sensation, your breath comes too quickly
    to speak,
Whilst Fanny was doing it for me I bit a piece out of her
    cheek;
And when you feel yourself spending and clasp it your legs in
    between,
O I should die if it ever got broken, God preserve the new
    Fucking Machine!

A new girl arrived, dearest Mary, and slept during last night
    with me;
When I put the machine to her cunny, she said 'None of that
    sort for me!'
She turned up her nose at our patent, and said we were
    'awfully green'
To injure ourselves with such habits, and not have the real
    Fucking Machine.
That all the men are all dying to have us, if only we'll give
    them the chance;
She was herself had in the carriage, coming home from the
    Lord Mayor's dance.
Now directly I get home next Xmas, I'll spoon my young
    cousin Jack Green,
And I swear he'll be only too ready, to lend me his Fucking
    Machine.

B

An airman told me ere he died,
I don't know if the bastard lied,
He said his wife had a cunt so wide,
She could never be satisfied.
So he made for her a prick of steel,
Attached by a crank to a bloody great wheel,
Two balls of brass he filled with cream,
And the whole ferking issue was driven by steam.
Round and round went the bloody great wheel,
In and out went the prick of steel,
Until in ecstasy she cried
'Stop it you buggers, I'm satisfied'
But here was a case of the biter bit,
There was no way of stopping it,
And so from arse to tit she split,
And the whole ferking issue was covered in shit.

C

An airman once before he died
(I don't know whether the bugger lied)
Said, however hard he tried
His wife was never satisfied.

96

So he fashioned her a prick of steel
Worked by a crank and a bloody great wheel,
Two brass balls were filled with cream,
And the whole bloody issue was driven by steam.
Round and round went the bloody great wheel,
In and out went the prick of steel,
Till, in ecstasy, she cried
'Stop! at last I'm satisfied.'
But this was a tale of the biter bit,
There was no way of stopping it,
She was from cunt to arsehole split,
And the whole fucking issue was covered in shit.

47. Furze Field

The female body is frequently poeticised as a lusciously inviting landscape, as in this rural song taken down by George Gardiner in 1907.

I have got a furze field, my own dearest jewel,
Where all my fine pheasants do fly,
And if you comes a-shooting when shooting's in season
I'll tell you, love, how to proceed.
You bring your dog with you, your gun in your hand,
All loaded and primed all at your command.
When the pheasants takes fright, you must take sight,
You shoot the next moment, you're sure to be right.

I have got a fishpond, my own dearest jewel,
Where all my fine fishes do play,
And if you comes a-fishing when fishing's in season
I'll tell you, love, how to proceed.
You bring your rod with you, your nets in your hand,
Your hooks and your angles all at your command.
When you throws in, all the fishes will play,
It's down to the bottom, and that's the right way.

I have got a warren, my own dearest jewel,
Where all my fine rabbits do play,
And if you comes a-ferreting when ferreting's in season
I'll tell you, love, how to proceed.
You bring your dog with you, your ferret in your hand,
Your hooks and your angles all at your command,
And the ferret will bolt and the rabbits will play,
For it's down to the bottom, and that's the right way.

48. Good Ship Venus

This possibly dates from the late Victorian period when Britain ruled the waves and almost everything else in sight; it is stylistically remarkable for using the limerick-stanza throughout. It became immensely popular as a navy song during World War Two.

A

On the good ship Venus
By God, you should have seen us,
The figurehead was a whore in bed
And the mast was a rampant penis.

The Captain of this lugger
Was Mark McAndrew Gugger;
He wasn't fit to shovel shit
The fornicating bugger.

The first Mate's name was Morgan,
He was a sexual Gorgon;
Ten times a day that man would play
Upon his sexual organ.

The second Mate was Walter,
At love he'd never falter,
The bloody stiff had given syph
To all the girls in Malta.

The third Mate was McGuire,
He really was a trier;
For when on shore he kept a whore,
On board he pulled his wire.

The Bos'n was some use to us,
He dipped his cock in phosphorus,
All through the night it kept alight
To guide us through the Bosphorus.

The Skipper's daughter Mabel
Whenever she was able

With the first mate would fornicate
Upon the cabin table.

The Skipper's younger daughter
Once fell into the water,
Delighted squeals revealed that eels
Had found her sexual quarter.

The baker's name was Farts,
He had tremendous parts;
He made a speciality
Of putting cream in tarts.

The cabin boy Agrippa,
A dirty little nipper,
Filled his arse with powdered glass
And circumcised the Skipper.

The crew were of savage races,
You could see it by their faces,
They started frigging against the rigging
For want of better places.

The ship's dog's name was Rover,
On board he was in clover,
They ground and ground that faithful hound
From Singapore to Dover.

On the China Station
We caused a great sensation
We sank a junk in seas of spunk
Through mutual masturbation.

And now I end this serial
For want of more material,
The ship and crew and Captain too
In hospital venereal.

B

Aboard the good ship Venus
By God you should have seen us:

The figurehead was a whore in bed
And the mast a rampant penis.
  Frigging in the rigging,
  Frigging in the rigging,
  Frigging in the rigging,
  'Cos there's fuck all else to do.

The Master's name was Morgan,
He was a sex-starved Gorgon;
Ten times a day he used to play
Upon his sexual organ.
  Frigging, &c.

The Captain's wife was Mabel,
Whenever she was able
She gave the crew their daily screw
Across the chart-room table.
  Frigging, &c.

When we put in to Calais
The Captain's daughter Sally,
Dressed as a whore, she rushed ashore
And won the Grand Prix rally.
  Frigging, &c.

The Captain's younger daughter
One day fell in the water;
Delighted squeals denoted eels
Had found her sexual quarter.
  Frigging, &c.

The cabin-boy was Nipper,
By God he was a ripper;
He stuffed his arse with broken glass
And circumcised the Skipper.
  Frigging, &c.

The Cook was called MacStrachen,
Each morning he would awaken
And scrape the spunk from off his bunk
To fry the Skipper's bacon.
  Frigging, &c.

His helper's name was Rudden,
By God he was a good 'un;
He tossed off twice in a bag of rice
And called it sago puddin'.
    Frigging, &c.

The ship's dog was called Rover,
His was no bed of clover;
We browned and browned that faithful hound
From Calais 'cross to Dover.
    Frigging, &c.

When in the Adriatic
The crew were quite ecstatic;
The rise and fall of cock and ball
Were purely automatic.
    Frigging, &c.

By careful navigation
We reached the China Station
And sunk a junk in a wave of spunk
By mutual masturbation.
    Frigging, &c.

C

'Twas on the Good Ship Venus,
By Christ, you should have seen us:
The figurehead was a whore in bed,
The mast was a rampant penis!
    So away, away with the fife and drum!
    Here we come, full o' rum!
    Lookin' for women who peddle their bum
    In the North Atlantic Squadron.

The captain's daughter Mabel,
By Christ was she ever able!
She gave the crew their daily screw
Across the galley table!
    So away, &c.

The captain loved the cabin-boy,
He loved him like a brother
And every night by candlelight
They bung-holed one another!
 So away, &c.

The cabin-boy, the cabin-boy,
The dirty little nipper:
He filled his ass with broken glass
And circumcised the skipper.
 So away, &c.

D

It was the Good Ship Venus,
My God you should have seen us:
A whore in bed was her figurehead
And her mast was a rampant penis.

The skipper's little daughter,
She fell into the water:
Delighted squeals soon showed that eels
Had found her sexual quarter.

His other daughter Mabel
Whenever she was able
Would fornicate with the second mate
Upon the cloakroom table.

The ship's boy's name was Nick,
A dirty little nipper:
He stuffed his arse with broken glass
And circumcised the skipper.

49. Green Grow the Rashes O

Burns collected this (the A-text exists in his holograph) and it was included in the *c.* 1800 *MMC*; the A-text seems to be the genuine oral article, the B-text was possibly worked over by Burns.

A

In sober hours I am a priest;
   A hero when I'm tipsey, O;
But I'm a king and ev'ry thing,
   When wi' a wanton Gipsey, O.
   Green grow the rashes O,
   Green grow the rashes O,
   The lasses they hae wimble-bores,   small holes
   The widows they hae gashes O.

'Twas late yestreen I met wi' ane,
   An' wow, but she was gentle, O!
Ae han' she pat roun' my cravat,
   The tither to my pintle, O.
   Green grow, &c.

I dought na speak – yet was na fley'd –
   My heart play'd duntie, duntie, O;
An' ceremony laid aside,
   I fairly fun' her cuntie, O.
   Green grow, &c.

B

O wat ye ought o' fisher Meg,
   And how she trow'd the webster, O,   rolled over/weaver
She loot me see her carrot cunt,
   And sell'd it for a labster, O.
   Green grow the rashes, O,
   Green grow the rashes, O,
   The lassies they hae wimble-bores,   small holes
   The widows they hae gashes, O.

Mistress Mary cow'd her thing   *cropped*
   Because she wad be gentle, O,
And span the fleece upon a rock
   To waft a Highland mantle, O.
   Green grow, &c.

An' heard ye o' the coat o' arms
   The Lyon brought our lady, O,
The crest was, couchant, sable cunt.
   The motto – 'ready, ready' O.
   Green grow, &c.

An' ken ye Leezie Lundie, O.
   The godly Leezie Lundie, O,
She mowes like reek thro' a' the week,   *fucks*
   But finger fucks on Sunday, O.
   Green grow, &c.

50. Hermit

A twentieth-century song still current in the oral repertoire and unusual for its reticence.

There once was a hermit who lived in a dell
I'll swear to the truth of the story I tell
My grandfather's grandfather knew him right well
This old hermit

He lived all alone at the side of a lake
Concoctions from nuts and from berries he'd make
Of nought but a fish would the good man partake
On a Friday

His hair was all matted and tattered his clothes
He once a year bathed his body unclothed
How the lake stood it the Lord only knows
He ain't saying

One morning in June he rose dripping and wet
When his horrified gaze two young ladies met
In feminine matters he was no vet
So he blushed

He grabbed for his hat as it lay on the beach
To cover up all that its broad rim would reach
Then he let out a horrified screech
Go away

The maids only laughed at his pitiful plight
And begged him to show them the wondrous sight
But he held to his hat and clutched it real tight
Just to cover it

Just at that moment a wandering gnat
Made the old man forget what he was at
He swatted the insect and let go the hat
Oh horrors

Now I have come to the crux of my tale
First he turned red and then he turned pale
He offered up a prayer and prayers never fail
So 'tis said

The end of my story leaves no doubt at all
That the Lord heard his prayer and answered his call
For he let go the hat but the hat didn't fall
Blessed miracle

51. Heroes

Mussolini invaded Abyssinia/Ethiopia in 1935; this item, sung to the tune of 'The British Grenadiers', was apparently circulated by the Ministry of Information during World War Two as a psychological weapon. In *A.P.H. His Life and Times* (London 1970, pp. 64-5), Sir Alan Herbert claimed to have met the original author: 'During War Two, one night at Hole Haven, I was talking to an R.N.V.R. officer . . . He shyly showed me some verses he said he had written about some things that Mussolini had done to the Abyssinians, and asked for my professional advice. I said I should not wish to alter a word. They were clever and decently abusive, and, given the theme, I should by no means have been ashamed of them.' Such are the vagaries of oral transmission that, within days, the poem was being confidently attributed to Sir Alan himself (cf. note to No. 100).

A

The Duce gives the order
To march against the foe
And off to darkest Africa
The organ-grinders go.

And now they are incapable
Of any kind of grind
For they're back from darkest Africa
With their organs left behind.

While the hosts of Abyssinia
Defending hearth and home
Have knick-knacks for the mantelpiece
Imported straight from Rome.

The Duce mounts the rostrum
On the warriors' return
With the unknown eunuch's ashes
In an old Etruscan urn.

'For some real act of gratitude
This great occasion calls,
What shall we give our heroes?'
And the heroes answered 'Balls'.

B
Il Duce gives the order
To go and fight the foe,
So off to Abyssinia
His organ-grinders go.

But now they can't participate
In any sort of grind,
For they're back from Abyssinia
With their organs left behind.

The Ethiopian warrior
Returns to hearth and home
With knick-knacks on the mantelpiece
Imported straight from Rome.

The Pope is inundated
With requests to join the choir
By his returning warriors
With voices octaves higher.

Il Duce mounts the rostrum
And to his people calls
'What shall we give our Generals?'
And the people answer 'Balls'.

52. Ho Boy

A straightforward expression of desire from *Pills*.

Ho boy, hey boy,
Come, come away boy,
    And bring me my longing desire;
A lass that is neat and can well do the feat
    When lusty young blood is on fire.

Let her body be tall,
And her waist be small,
    And her age not above eighteen;
Let her care for no bed but here let spread
    Her mantle upon the green.

Let her face be fair
And her breasts be bare,
    And a voice let her have that can warble;
Let her belly be soft but to mount me aloft
    Let her bounding buttocks be marble.

Let her have a cherry lip
Where I nectar may sip
    Let her eyes be as black as a sloe;
Dangling locks I do love so that those hang above
    Are the same with what grows below.

O such a bonny lass
May bring wonders to pass,
    And make me grow younger and younger;
And when'er we do part, she'll be mad at the heart
    That I'm able to tarry no longer.

53. Hole in the Elephant's Bottom

An early twentieth-century music-hall dirge on hard times in the acting profession.

I wanted to go on the stage,
And now my ambition I've gotten:
In pantomime I'm all the rage
As the hole in the elephant's bottom.

My manager says it's all balls,
He claims that my acting is rotten;
I wave to the girls in the stalls
Through the hole in the elephant's bottom.

My part hasn't got any words,
If it had I'd most likely forgot 'em;
I simply drop property turds
Through the hole in the elephant's bottom.

My landlady packs up my meals,
One day I went out and forgot 'em;
So at matinee they fed me my tea
Through the hole in the elephant's bottom.

Two nancy boys came on one day,
Though the manager tried hard to stop 'em;
They passed me a lovely bouquet
Through the hole in the elephant's bottom.

The elephant's bollocks hang low
And part of my job is to knot 'em:
I tie them up tight in a bow
Through the hole in the elephant's bottom.

54. Hymn of Sorrow

Sung – to the tune of 'Clementine' or 'Deutschland Uber Alles' – by servicemen in World War Two. Its cheery acceptance of adversity suggests a POW camp origin.

A

Life presents a dismal picture,
Pregnant with impending doom:
Father has an anal stricture,
Mother has a fallen womb;

Sister Lucy's been aborted
For the forty-second time;
Brother Bertie's been deported
For a homosexual crime;

And the kid is just another,
Always having bloody fits,
Every time it coughs it vomits,
Every time it farts it shits;

Yet we face the future fearless
Although fortune rarely smiles,
My new job is cold and cheerless –
Chipping ice for Grandpa's piles;

No! We are not broken-hearted,
Neither are we up the spout!
Grandmama this moment farted,
Blew her arsehole inside out.

B

Home presents a dismal picture,
Dark and silent as the tomb;
Father has an anal stricture,
Mother has a fallen womb.

But we are not yet downhearted,
Neither are we up the spout;

Auntie Mabel has just farted,
Blew her arsehole inside out.

Uncle Max has been deported
For a homosexual crime;
Sister Grace has been aborted
For the forty-seventh time.

But we are not yet downhearted,
Neither are we up the spout;
Auntie Mabel has just farted,
Blew her arsehole inside out.

C

Listen to my tale of sorrow
Of our fast-approaching doom:
Father's got an anal stricture,
Mother's got a palsied womb;

Sister Lucy's been aborted
For the forty-second time;
Brother Bertie's been deported
For a homosexual crime.

Sister Gerty's monthly periods
Flood the countryside for miles;
My new job is cold and cheerless –
Chipping ice for Grandpa's piles.

D

Ours is a dark and dreary household,
Dark and dreary as the tomb:
Father's got a pelvic rupture,
Mother's got a fallen womb.

Little Brother's been deported
For a homosexual crime,
And the housemaid's just aborted
For the forty-second time.

But we must not be downhearted,
We must not be put about,
Auntie Mary has just farted
And turned her arsehole inside out.

55. I Dreamed My Love

A bawdy dream-poem from Percy's Folio MS (see headnote to No. 5).

I dreamed my love lay in her bed
   And 'twas my chance to take her.
Her arms and legs abroad were spread.
   She slept, I durst not wake her.

O pity it were that one so fair
   Should crown her head with willow.
The tresses of her golden hair
   Did kiss her lovely pillow.

Me thought her belly was a hill
   Much like a mount of pleasure,
At foot whereof there springs a well,
   The depth no man can measure.

About the pleasant mountain head
   There grew a lovely thicket,
Whither two beagles travelled
   And raised a lively pricket.

They hunted him with cheerful cry
   About this pleasant mountain,
That he with heat was forced to fly
   And slip into the fountain.

Those beagles followed to the brink
   And there at him they baited.
He plunged about but would not shrink.
   His coming-forth they waited.

Then forth he came as one half lame,
   Full weary, faint and tired,
And laid him down between her legs
   As help he had required.

Those beagles being refreshed again,
    My love from sleep bereaved.
She dreamed she had me in her arms
    And she was not deceived.

56. I Wish I Was

A product of the aptly named Hungry Thirties, it has, despite the melancholy tone, survived in the oral tradition to the present.

I wish I was a fascinating bitch,
I'd never be poor; I'd always be rich.
I'd sleep all day and I'd work all night,
I'd always do wrong and always be right.
And once a month I'd take a rest,
To make all my customers wild;
Oh, I wish I was a fascinating bitch
And not an illegitimate child,
And not an illegitimate child.

57. Jack and Jill

The apparent innocence of nursery rhymes presents an irresistible target for the bawdy muse as this modern parody demonstrates.

Jack and Jill went up a hill
To fetch a pail of water;
Jill came down with half a crown
But not for carrying water.

58. John Anderson My Jo

One of the great oral products of the world, it was used by
Burns as the model for his celebrated song of the same name,
and collected in the *c*. 1800 *MMC*. The mixture of poignancy
with sexual pain, the majestic movement of the verse, and the
clarity of the imagery all make it unforgettable.

John Anderson, my jo, John,
   I wonder what ye mean,
To lie sae lang i' the mornin',
   And sit sae late at e'en?
Ye'll bleer a' your een, John,
   And why do ye so?
Come sooner to your bed at een,
   John Anderson, my jo.

John Anderson, my jo, John,
   When first that ye began,
Ye had as good a tail-tree,
   As ony ither man;
But now it's waxen wan, John,
   And wrinkles to and fro;
I've twa gae-ups for ae gae-down,
   John Anderson, my jo.

I'm backit like a salmon,
   I'm breastit like a swan;
My wame it is a down-cod,   *belly/feather pillow*
   My middle ye may span:
Frae my tap-knot to my tae, John,
   I'm like the new-fa'n snow;
And it's a' for your convenience,
   John Anderson, my jo.

O it is a fine thing
   To keep out o'er the dyke;   *watch out*
But it is a meikle finer thing,
   To see your hurdies fyke;   *buttocks jerk*

To see your hurdies fyke, John,
   And hit the rising blow;
It's then I like your chanter-pipe,
   John Anderson, my jo.

When ye come on before, John,
   See that ye do your best;
When ye begin to haud me
   See that ye grip me fast;
See that ye grip me fast, John,
   Until that I cry 'Oh!'
Your back shall crack or I do that,
   John Anderson, my jo.

John Anderson, my jo, John,
   Ye're welcome when ye please;
It's either in the warm bed
   Or else aboon the claes:
Or ye shall hae the horns, John,
   Upon your head to grow;
An' that's the cuckold's mallison,   *curse*
   John Anderson, my jo.

59. Johnie Scott

A tale of sartorial improvisation collected by Burns and printed in the *c.* 1800 *MMC*.

Whare will we get a coat to Johnie Scott,
    Amang us maidens a'?
Whare will we get a coat to Johnie Scott,
    To mak the laddie braw:

There's your cunt hair, and there's my cunt hair,
    An' we'll twine it wondrous sma';
An' if waft be scarce, we'll cowe our arse,   *crop*
    To mak him kilt an' a'.

60. Kathoozalem

Parodies a song of 1866 in which the Baba of Jerusalem used a cord greased with goozalem to garrotte his daughter and her infidel lover. Still popular in universities because of the student-hero.

A

In Judah's shade there lived a maid –
A prostitute, a renegade,
A Mistress of the whoring trade –
Her name it was Kathoozalem.
  Hi-ho Kathoozalem,
  Kathoozalem, Kathoozalem,
  Hi-ho Kathoozalem,
  The harlot of Jerusalem.

A student lived beneath the wall;
Although he'd only got one ball
He'd been through all or nearly all
The harlots in Jerusalem.
  Hi-ho, &c.

One night – returning from a spree –
Although he couldn't raise the fee
He whistled as was customary
And crossed the fair Kathoozalem.
  Hi-ho, &c.

He led her to a shady nook
And from beneath his cloak he took
A penis like a shepherd's crook:
The pride of all Jerusalem.
  Hi-ho, &c.

He laid her gently on her bum
And, squirting like a Maxim Gun,
He sowed the seed of many a son
Within the fair Kathoozalem.
  Hi-ho, &c.

When up there strolled an Israelite –
A Jebusite, a bloody shite –
Who thought that he would spend the night
Within the fair Kathoozalem.
  Hi-ho, &c.

He gave the pair a dirty look
Then grabbed the student by his crook
And hurled him into Canaan's Brook
That flows hard by Jerusalem.
  Hi-ho, &c.

The student got up full of fight;
He grabbed that fucking Jebusite
And rammed him up with all his might
The arsehole of Kathoozalem.
  Hi-ho, &c.

The wily whore she knew her part,
She held her breath and blew a fart
That blew him straight as any dart
Out across Jerusalem.
  Hi-ho, &c.

He flew out high across the sea –
It was the sea of Galilee –
And hitched his balls upon a tree
That grows outside Jerusalem.
  Hi-ho, &c.

So now then all you randy folk
Who love to have your nightly poke:
Just pay the fee and let it soak
Within the fair Kathoozalem.
  Hi-ho, &c.

B

In days of yore there lived a whore,
A prostitute of low repute,
Who did a roaring whoring trade –
The harlot of Jerusalem.

Heigh-ho Kathoozalem,
Kathoozalem, Kathoozalem;
Heigh-ho Kathoozalem,
The harlot of Jerusalem.

There lived a student by the wall;
Although he only had one ball
He'd screwed the harlots one and all
That lived by fair Jerusalem.
   Heigh-ho, &c.

One night, returning from the spree
With his accustomed jollity,
Although he hadn't paid the fee
He crossed the fair Kathoozalem.
   Heigh-ho, &c.

He took her to a shady nook
And from beneath his cloak he took
His penis like a shepherd's crook,
The pride of all Jerusalem.
   Heigh-ho, &c.

He laid her down upon her bum
And, shooting like a Maxim Gun,
He sowed the seed of many a son
Within the fair Kathoozalem.
   Heigh-ho, &c.

But up there came an Israelite –
A Jebusite, a bloody shite –
And he had vowed to spend the night
Within the fair Kathoozalem.
   Heigh-ho, &c.

He seized the student by his hook
And with a mighty heave he took
And threw him over Canaan's Brook
That flows hard by Jerusalem.
   Heigh-ho, &c.

That student he was full of fight:
He seized the Jew, that bloody shite,
And stuffed him up with all his might
The arse of fair Kathoozalem.
    Heigh-ho, &c.

That comely tart she knew her part,
She squeezed her cunt and blew a fart
That blew him straight as any dart
High across Jerusalem.
    Heigh-ho, &c.

She blew him o'er the deep blue sea –
It was the sea of Galilee –
He caught his balls upon a tree
That grew above Jerusalem.
    Heigh-ho, &c.

So here's to all you gentle folk
Who love to have your nightly poke;
May you often let it soak
Within the fair Kathoozalem.
    Heigh-ho, &c.

61. Keyhole in the Door

Gershon Legman informs me in a letter of 3 January 1979: 'This was sung on American whaling-ships as an entertainment song in the 1870s (have found a logbook containing a rather polite form); bawdier forms proliferated since about 1888. The form in which, at the end, the man puts his penis *into* the keyhole (and sometimes gets v.d. from it!) is a recent travesty.'

I took my love home early,
'Twas just on half past nine,
And by some stroke of bloody good luck,
Her room was next to mine.
Like Christopher Columbus
I decided to explore
And took up my position by
The keyhole in the door.
   Oh the keyhole, keyhole, keyhole, keyhole,
   Keyhole in the door,
   And took up my position by
   The keyhole in the door.

My love sat by the fireside,
Her little feet to warm,
With only a lilywhite chemise
To cover her lovely form.
Thought I if she would take it off
I'd ask for nothing more,
By Christ I saw her do it,
Through the keyhole in the door.
   Oh the keyhole, &c.

With trembling hands and fingers,
I tapped upon the door
And after some persuasion
I crossed the threshold o'er;
To prevent others seeing
What I had seen before,

I stuffed that lilywhite chemise
Through the keyhole in the door.
    Oh the keyhole, &c.

That night I slept in clover,
And something else beside,
And on that bouncing bosom
Had many a joyful ride.
When I awoke next morning,
My prick was red and raw,
As if I'd been and stuffed
Through the keyhole in the door.
    Oh the keyhole, &c.

62. Last Night I Lay in Bed

The opening of the Neapolitan Funicular Railway was celebrated in Denza's 'Funiculi Funicula' (1880). By the 1920s the song had become so contemptibly familiar that some anonymous amateur produced this parody.

Last night I lay in bed and pulled my plonker,
It did me good, I knew it would,
Tonight I shall repeat the operation,
I'll do it twice, it's very nice!

First I'll give it the long strokes,
Up and down, up and down,
Then I'll give it the short strokes,
Around and round, around and round.

Bash it, thrash it, beat it on the floor!
Smite it, bite it, jam it in the door!
Some say that buggery is grand,
Some claim that fucking's good,
But for personal satisfaction
I prefer to pull my pud!

63. Long Peggin' Awl

An awl is a tradesman's tool for boring small holes, so it became an inevitable sexual metaphor; this nineteenth-century song celebrates the persuasive power of the tool.

As I was a-walking one morning in May,
I met a pretty fair maid, her gown it was gay.
I stepped up to her and back she did fall.
She wanted to be played with the long peggin' awl.

I said, 'Pretty fair maid, will you travel with me
Unto foreign countries strange things for to see?
And I will protect you whate'er may befall,
And follow your love with his long peggin' awl.'

Then home to her parents she then went straightway,
And unto her mother these words she did say:
'I'll follow my true love, whate'er may befall,
I'll follow my love with his long peggin' awl.'

'O daughter, o daughter, how can you say so?
For young men are false, you very well know.
They'll tell you fine things and the devil and all,
And leave you big-bellied with the long peggin' awl.'

'O mother, o mother, now do not say so.
Before you were sixteen you very well know,
There was father and mother and baby and all.
You followed my dad for his long peggin' awl.'

64. Lulu

Frank Wedekind's dramas *Erdgeist* (1895) and *Die Büchse der Pandora* (1904) – and Alban Berg's unfinished serial opera *Lulu* (1928–35) based on them – made the name Lulu synonymous with the *femme fatale*. In these great works Lulu ends as a prostitute who is eventually murdered by Jack the Ripper; the popular Lulu of twentieth-century bawdry avoids the histrionic sticky end but has a similar compelling charm.

Some girls work in factories,
And some girls work in stores,
But Lulu works in a knocking shop
With forty other whores.
    Bang it into Lulu,
    Bang it good and strong;
    What shall we do for a bloody good screw
    When Lulu's dead and gone?

I've seen rings of silver,
And I've seen rings of brass,
But the finest rings I ever did see
Were the rings up Lulu's arse.
    Bang it, &c.

I wish I were a ring
On Lulu's lovely hand,
'Cos every time she wiped her arse
I'd see the promised land.
    Bang it, &c.

Now Lulu had a baby,
It gave her quite a shock,
She couldn't call it Lulu,
'Cos the bastard had a cock.
    Bang it, &c.

Lulu had another,
She called it Sunny Jim,

She couldn't call it Lulu
'Cos the bugger had no quim.
    Bang it, &c.

I wish I were a pisspot
Beneath my Lulu's bed,
Then every time she took it out
I'd see her maidenhead.
    Bang it, &c.

I took her to the swimming baths,
Where Lulu tried to swim,
But every time she opened her legs
The water guggled in.
    Bang it, &c.

65. Lusty Blacksmith

When a popular song is fixed in print the possibility of it changing in oral transmission is accordingly diminished; the A-text is a broadside of 1705, the B-text was learned orally during World War Two.

A

A lusty young smith at his vice stood a filing,
Rub, rub, rub, rub, rub, rub in and out, in and out ho;
When to him a buxom young damsel came smiling,
And asked if to work at her forge he would go;
   With a rub, rub, rub, rub, rub, rub in and out, in and out ho.

'A match,' quoth the smith, so away they went thither
Rub, rub, rub, rub, rub, rub in and out, in and out ho;
They stripped to go to't, 'twas hot work and hot weather,
She kindled a fire, and soon made him blow;
   With a rub, &c.

Red-hot grew his iron as both did desire,
And he was too wise not to strike while 'twas so;
Quoth she, 'What I get, I get out of the fire,
Then prithee strike home and redouble the blow.'
   With a rub, &c.

Six times did his iron by vigorous heating,
Grow soft in the forge for a minute or so;
As often 'twas hardened, still beating and beating,
But the more it was softened it hardened more slow:
   With a rub, &c.

The smith then would go, quoth the dame full of sorrow,
'Oh what would I give, could my cuckold do so!
Good lad with your hammer come hither tomorrow,
But pray can't you use it once more e'er you go?'
   With a rub, &c.

B

A lusty young smith at his vice stood a filing,
His hammer laid by, but his forge stood aglow,
When to him a buxom young woman came smiling
And asked if to work at her forge he would go.
With a jingle-bang, jingle-bang, jingle-bang-jingle,
With a jingle-bang, jingle-bang-jingle, Hey-ho.

'I will,' said the smith, and they went off together,
Along to the young woman's house they did go.
They stripped to go to it, 'twas hot work in hot weather,
But she kindled a fire and she soon made him glow.
With a jingle-bang, &c.

Her husband, she said, no good work could afford her;
His strength and his tools were worn out long ago.
The smith said, 'Well, mine are in very good order,
And now I am ready my skill for to show.'
With a jingle-bang, &c.

Red hot grew his iron as both did desire,
And he was too wise not to strike while 'twas so.
Quoth she, 'What I get, I get out of the fire,
So prithee strike home and redouble the blow.'
With a jingle-bang, &c.

Six times did his iron by vigorous heating
Grow soft in the forge in a minute or so,
But each time it hardened, still beating and beating,
But the more it was softened it hardened more slow.
With a jingle-bang, &c.

The smith then would go; said the dame, full of sorrow,
'Oh what would I give could my husband do so!
Young man with your hammer come hither tomorrow
But pray can't you use it once more ere you go?'
With a jingle-bang, &c.

66. Madgie Cam to My Bed-stock

Collected by Burns and printed in the *c.* 1800 *MMC*. In *Burns Today and Tomorrow*, Edinburgh 1959, p. 50, Hugh MacDiarmid wrote that W. B. Yeats considered this 'one of the finest obscene poems he had ever heard'.

Madgie cam to my bed-stock,
   To see gif I was waukin';
I pat my han' atweesh her feet,
   An' fand her wee bit maukin.   *hare*

Cunt it was the sowen-pat,   *gruel pot*
   An' pintle was the ladle;
Ballocks were the serving-men
   That waited at the table.

67. Maiden's Wish

An authoritative metrical discourse from *The Pearl* (4 October 1879).

When wishes first enter a maiden's breast
She longs by her lover to be caressed;
She longs with her lover to do the trick,
And in secret she longs for a taste of his prick!
Her cunt it is itching from morning till night,
The prick of her lover can yield her delight,
She longs to be fucked and for that does deplore,
For what can a young maiden wish for more?

If fever or sickness her spirits doth shock,
Why we know what she wants, 'tis a stiff standing cock!
Give her a prick, it will soon make her well,
Though perhaps in the long run her belly may swell!
She'd like very well to be laid on the grass,
To have two ample bollocks sent bang 'gainst her arse,
She longs to be fucked and for that does deplore,
For what can a young maiden wish for more?

It's a pity any quim hungry should do,
All maids wish them filled, as you very well know,
And if the young men would be ready and free,
They'd up with their clouts in a trice, d'ye see!
She wants to be asked, but to ask is afraid,
And fearful she is, that she'll die an old maid;
She wishes for prick, and for that does deplore,
For what can a young maiden wish for more?

68. Mary

In World War One the war effort of countless women gained the sex immense respect and, eventually, the vote; this is a bawdy aside on the matter.

Mary in the kitchen pummelling duff
Cheeks of her arse go Puff Puff Puff
   O Puff.

Mary in the coal hole shovelling coal
Finger up the chief engineer's arsehole
   O coal.

Mary in the shithouse shovelling shit
Syphilitic chancre on her starboard tit
   O shit.

69. Ma's Out

The bawdy impulse is reduced to the level of playful naughtiness in this twentieth-century catchphrase.

Ma's out, Pa's out,
Let's talk dirt:

Pee, po, belly, bottom,
Bum, fart, drawers.

70. Meeting

From *Pills*; in bawdy poetry death is always a euphemism for orgasm so when the girl talks of 'the slaughter' she anticipates a sexual triumph.

As I went o'er yon misty moor
   'Twas on an evening late, Sir,
There I met with a welfared lass
   Was spanning of her gate, Sir;
I took her by the lillywhite hand
   And by the twat I caught her,
I swear and vow and tell you true
   She pissed in my hand with laughter.

The silly poor wench she lay so still
   You'd swear she had been dead, Sir,
The deel a word but 'aw' she said, but 'ay',
   And bowed her head, Sir;
'Kind Sir,' quoth she, 'you'll kill me here,
   But I'll forget the slaughter,
You make such motions with your arse
   You'll split my sides with laughter.'

71. Mobile

The prosperous Alabama seaport of Mobile has become in-
famous in this twentieth-century American bawdy song which
goes to the tune of 'Coming Round the Mountain', and
emerged after the Spanish-American war of 1898.

O the eagles they fly high in Mobile!
O the eagles they fly high in Mobile!
O the eagles they fly high and they shit right in your eye
It's a good job they don't fly in Mobile.
  In Mobile! In Mobile!
  In Mo- In Mo- In Mo- In Mobile!
  O the eagles they fly high and they shit right in your eye
  It's a good job cows don't fly in Mobile!

There's a shortage of good whores in Mobile!
There's a shortage of good whores in Mobile!
There's a shortage of good whores but there's keyholes in the
    doors
And there's knotholes in the floors in Mobile!
  In Mobile, &c.

There's a lack of fornication in Mobile!
There's a lack of fornication in Mobile!
There's a lack of fornication but there's lots of masturbation
What a bloody situation in Mobile!
  In Mobile, &c.

There's no paper in the bogs in Mobile!
There's no paper in the bogs in Mobile!
There's no paper in the bogs so they wait until it clogs
Then they saw it off in logs in Mobile!
  In Mobile, &c.

O the women wear tin pants in Mobile!
O the women wear tin pants in Mobile!
O the women wear tin pants but they take 'em off to dance
Then every bugger gets his chance in Mobile!
  In Mobile, &c.

There's an ugly dame called Dinah in Mobile!
There's an ugly dame called Dinah in Mobile!
There's an ugly dame called Dinah but if you ask the guys
    who grind her
They'll say she's got the best vagina in Mobile!
   In Mobile, &c.

There are seagulls round the lighthouse in Mobile!
There are seagulls round the lighthouse in Mobile!
There are seagulls round the lighthouse and the lighthouse is
    a white house
'Cos they use it as a shite house in Mobile!
   In Mobile, &c.

Members of the working classes in Mobile!
Members of the working classes in Mobile!
Members of the working classes when they've finished with
    their glasses
They just stuff them up their asses in Mobile!
   In Mobile, &c.

O I met the parson's daughter in Mobile!
O I met the parson's daughter in Mobile!
O I met the parson's daughter, caught her, fought her, sought
    her, taught her,
Felt her, fucked her, stopped her water in Mobile!
   In Mobile, &c.

72. Modiewark

In this song – collected by Burns and printed in the *c.* 1800 *MMC* – the mole joins the ferret as an animal sex symbol.

The modiewark has done me ill,   *mole*
And below my apron has biggit a hill;
I maun consult some learned clark
About this wanton modiewark.
   An' O the wanton modiewark,
   The weary wanton modiewark;
   I maun consult some learned clark
   About this wanton modiewark.

O first it gat between my taes,
Out o'er my garter niest it gaes;   *next*
At length it crap below my sark,   *shift*
The weary wanton modiewark.
   An' O, &c.

This modiewark, tho' it be blin';
If ance its nose you lat it in,
Then to the hilts, within a crack
It's out o' sight, the modiewark.
   An' O, &c.

When Marjorie was made a bride,
An' Willy lay down by her side,
Syne nocht was hard, when a' was dark,
But kicking at the modiewark.
   An' O, &c.

73. Mower

The agricultural ritual of mowing has an obvious sexual connotation that has long been exploited in folksong; the A-text (from the Rawlinson MS, Poet. 216) dates from the beginning of the seventeenth century, the B-text is a nineteenth-century broadside.

A

Down in the meadow, the river running clear,
'Twas in the month of July, the prime time of the year,
When many pretty little fishes in the brooks did play,
And many a lad and many a lass, abroad a-making hay.

In came the mower, to mow the meadows down,
With his bag and bottle, with ale that was so brown:
He took his scythe with a courage bold, and looking in the sky,
He sighed, he mowed, he swived, he blowed; the grass rubs
      very dry.

'Salt seasons all things!' quoth Solomon the wise;
And she that hath a fat cunt would make a prick rise;
But she that hath a lean one and never a jot of hair,—
The devil take her napping, as Moss did his mare.

B

It was one summer's morning on the fourteenth day of May,
I met a fair maid, she asked my trade, I made her this reply,
'For by my occupation I ramble up and down,
With my taring scythe in order to mow the meadows down.'

She said, 'My handsome young man, if a mower that you be,
I'll find you some new employment if you will go with me,
For I have a little meadow long kept for you in store,
It was on the dew, I tell you true, it ne'er was cut before.'

He said, 'My pretty fair maid, if it is as you say,
I'll do my best endeavours in cutting of your hay,
For in your lovely countenance I never saw a frown,

So my lovely lass, I'll cut your grass, that's ne'er been
    trampled down.'

With courage bold undaunted she took him to the ground,
With his taring scythe in hand to mow the meadow down;
He mowed from nine till breakfast time, so far beyond his
    skill,
He was forced to yield and quit the field, for the grass was
    growing still.

She says, 'My handsome young man, you did promise me and
    say
You'd do your best endeavours in cutting of the hay,
For in my little meadow, you'll ne'er find hills nor rocks,
So I pray young man don't leave me, till you see my hay in
    cocks.'

He said, 'My pretty fair maid, I can no longer stay,
But I'll go to Newry, in cutting of the hay,
But if I find the grass is cut in the country where I go,
It's then perhaps I may return, your meadow for to mow.'

Now her hay being in order, and harvest being all o'er,
This young man's gone and left her sad case for to deplore,
But where he's gone I do not know, so far beyond my skill,
I was forced to yield and quit the field, for grass is growing
    still.

74. Muirland Meg

Collected by Burns (it exists in his holograph) and printed in the *c.* 1800 *MMC* this must have greatly appealed to the poet who was always ready to respond to the lass who gave 'gude measure'.

Among our young lassies there's Muirland Meg,
She'll beg or she work, and she'll play or she beg,
At thirteen her maidenhead flew to the gate,
And the door o' her cage stands open yet.
    And for a sheep-cloot she'll do't, she'll do't,   *sheep's foot*
    And for a sheep-cloot she'll do't;
    And for a toop-horn she'll do't to the morn,   *ram's horn*
    And merrily turn and do't, and do't.

Her kittle black een they wad thirl you thro'.   *dangerous/thrill*
Her rose-bud lips cry, kiss me now;
The curls and links o' her bonie black hair,
Wad put you in mind that the lassie has mair.
    And for a sheep-cloot, &c.

An armfu' o' love is her bosom sae plump,
A span o' delight is her middle sae jimp;   *slender*
A taper, white leg, and a thumpin thie,
And a fiddle near by, an ye play a wee!
    And for a sheep-cloot, &c.

Love's her delight, and kissin's her treasure;
She'll stick at nae price, and ye gie her gude measure,
As lang's a sheep-fit, and as girt's a goose-egg,   *sheep-foot/large*
And that's the measure o' Muirland Meg.
    And for a sheep-cloot, &c.

75. My Mistress

The encomium was immensely popular during the seventeenth century though here the praise is qualified by suspicion; the A-text is from the Rawlinson MS (Poet. 26), the B-text from *Pills*.

A

My mistress is a shuttlecock
   Composed of cork and feather.
Each battledore plays on her dock
   And bandies on her leather.
And one will not suffice her will;
She flies unto another still.

My mistress is a tennis-ball
   Composed of leather fine.
She's often banged against the wall
   And strucken under-line.
But he that means to win her will
Must hit her in the hazard still.

My mistress is a tinder-box.
   Would I had such a one!
Her steel endureth many knocks,
   Being struck against the stone.
But if you stir her tinder much
Your match will fire with a touch.

My mistress is a ship of war.
   Much shot is discharged at her.
Her poop receiveth many a scar
   To bear 'twixt wind and water.
But where she grapples, at the last
She sinks and striketh down his mast.

My mistress is a nightingale,
   So sweetly can she sing.
She is as fair as Philomel,
   The daughter of a king.

And in the night and darkness thick
She loves to lean against a prick.

My mistress is a warrior's tent,
   A lawyer's case is she,
A fiddler's knee-held instrument,
   A huntsman's venery.
A two-leaved book she's for the school,
A toying bauble for a fool.

But why do I my mistress call
   An instrument, a bauble?
A shuttlecock, a tennis-ball,
   A ship of war unstable?
Say but this and say no more:
She is a woman and a whore.

B

My mistress is a hive of bees
   In yonder flowery garden,
To her they come with loaden thighs,
   To ease them of their burden:
As under the beehive lieth the wax,
   And under the wax is honey,
So under her waist her belly is placed,
   And under that her cuny.

My mistress is a mine of gold,
   Would that it were her pleasure,
To let me dig within her mould,
   And roll among her treasure.
As under the moss the mould doth lie,
   And under the mould is money
So under her waist her belly is placed,
   And under that her cuny.

My mistress is a morn of May,
   Which drops of dew down stilleth,
Where e'er she goes to sport and play,
   The dew down sweetly trilleth,
As under the sun the mist doth lie,

So under the mist it is sunny,
So under her waist her belly is placed,
  And under that her cuny.

My mistress is a pleasant spring
  That yieldeth store of water sweet,
That doth refresh each withered thing
  Lies trodden under feet;
Her belly is both white and soft,
  And downy as any bunny,
That many gallants wish full oft
  To play but with her cuny.

My mistress hath the magic sprays,
  Of late she takes such wondrous pain,
That she can pleasing spirits raise,
  And also lay them down again,
Such power hath my tripping doe,
  My little pretty bunny,
That many would their lives forego,
  To play but with her cuny.

76. Nae Hair On't

A cautionary tale in the cause of premarital carnal knowledge, collected by Burns and printed in the *c.* 1800 *MMC*.

Yestreen I wed a lady fair,
  And ye wad believe me,
On her cunt there grows nae hair,
  That's the thing that grieves me.

It vexed me sair, it plagued me sair,
  It put me in a passion,
To think that I had wad a wife,
  Whase cunt was out o' fashion.

77. Never Wed an Old Man

Poets like Ovid (*Amores*, III, vii) and Rochester ('The Imperfect Enjoyment') have made memorable poetry from the theme of impotence; this folksong, popular since the nineteenth century, gives the female point of view.

For an aul' man come courtin' me,
Hi-doo-a-darrity,
An aul' man come courtin' me,
Hi-doo-a-day.
For an aul' man come courtin' me,
Hi-doo-a-darrity,
Maids, when you're young never wed a aul' man.

For when we went to the church,
I left him in the lurch,
When we went to the church,
Me being young,
When we went to the church
I left him in the lurch,
Maids, when you're young never wed a aul' man.

For when we went to oor tea
He started teasing me.
When we went to oor tea,
Me being young,
When we went to oor tea
He started teasing me,
Maids, when you're young never wed a aul' man.

When we went to oor bed
He lay as he was dead,
When we went to oor bed,
Me being young,
When we went to oor bed
He lay as he was dead,
Maids, when you're young never wed a aul' man.

For he has no tooralo,
Right-fol-the-dooralo,
He has no tooralo,
Right-fol-the-day;
For he has no tooralo
To full up my dooralo,
Maids, when you're young never wed a aul' man.

78. New Deal

A sturdy survivor, American in origin, from World War Two.

Hitler said 'More babies',
Musso said 'Me too';
But F.D.R. had a better plan
And this was what to do:
He put a ban on rubber
And set the clock ahead,
Then left the rest to Nature
And an extra hour in bed.

79. No Balls at All

Legman (p. 377) identifies this as a late nineteenth-century travesty 'set to the rhythms of a topical satire against excesses in women's clothing, "Nothing to Wear", by Wm. Allen Butler'; in World War Two its chorus expanded into the ubiquitous marching-song 'Hitler has only got one ball/ Goering has two but very small/Himmler has something similar/But poor old Goebbels has no balls at all'.

Come all you young maidens and listen to me,
I'll tell you a tale that will fill you with glee,
About a young maiden so fair and so small
Who married a man who had no balls at all.
  No balls at all, no balls at all:
  She married a man who had no balls at all.

On the night of her wedding she dived into bed,
Her breasts were all tingling, her legs were well spread,
She felt for his penis and found it was small
And then she discovered he had no balls at all.
  No balls, &c.

'O mother, dear mother, consider my luck –
I've married a man who's unable to fuck;
For many a year I've avoided the call,
Now I've married a man who has no balls at all.'
  No balls, &c.

'O daughter, dear daughter, don't take it so bad,
I had the same trouble with your dear old dad;
There are eager young men who will answer the call
Of the wife of a man who has no balls at all.'
  No balls, &c.

So the daughter took heed of her mother's advice,
And she found the results were exceedingly nice;
A bouncing young baby was born in the Fall,
But the poor little bastard had no balls at all.
  No balls, &c.

80. Nutting Girl

A nineteenth-century broadside containing an early use of nuts as a sexually provocative symbol.

Now come all you jovial fellows, come listen to my song,
It is a little ditty and it won't contain you long.
It's of a fair young damsel, she lived down in Kent,
Arose one summer's mornin', she a-nuttin' went.
   With my fal-lal to my ral-tal-lal,
   Sing whack fol the dear-ol-day,
   And what few nuts that poor girl had
   She threw them all away.

It's of a brisk young farmer was ploughing of his land,
He called unto his horses to bid them gently stand;
As he sit down upon his plough all for a song to sing,
His voice was so melodious it made the valleys ring.
   With my fal-lal, &c.

It's of this fair young damsel was nuttin' in a wood,
His voice was so melodious it charmed her as she stood.
She could no longer stay,
And what nuts she had, poor girl, she threw them all away.
   With my fal-lal, &c.

So then came to young Johnny as he sit on his plough,
She said, 'Young man I really feel I cannot tell you how.'
He took her to some shady broom, and there he laid her down,
Says she, 'Young man, I think I feel the world go round and
     round.'
   With my fal-lal, &c.

Now come all you young women, this warning by me take,
If you should a-nutting go, please get home in time,
For if you should stay too late to hear the ploughboy sing
You might have a young farmer to nurse up in the spring.
   With my fal-lal, &c.

81. O Dear What Can the Matter Be

A parody popular with troops in World War One and with children ever since.

O dear what can the matter be?
Three whores locked in a lavatory,
There all Friday and Saturday,
And nobody knew they were there.

The first whore was Miss Mary Croker,
First satisfied by a big Irish stoker,
He did the job with a red heatened poker
And she didn't know it was there.
    O dear, &c.

The second whore was Miss Mabel Porter,
Now she was the Bishop of Chichester's daughter,
She came there to piss off superfluous water
And nobody knew she was there.
    O dear, &c.

The third whore was Miss Penelope Carter,
She was renowned as the world's greatest farter,
She'd fart any tune like the Moonlight Sonata
Yet nobody knew she was there.
    O dear, &c.

82. O No John

In his great period of folksong collecting in Somerset (1903–7) Cecil Sharp transcribed a version of this which subsequently became popular enough to be a subject fit for parody; the transformation of a rigid negative into a positive cry of ecstasy suggests art of a high order.

On yonder hill there lives a lady
Who she is I do not know;
I'll go woo her for her beauty,
She must answer Yes or No.
'Oh No John, No John, No John No!'

Her husband is a Spanish Captain,
Went to sea a year ago;
First he loved her, then he left her,
Bade her always answer 'No'.
'Oh No John, No John, No John No!'

'Madam on your cheek are roses,
In your eyes blue violets grow;
Will you take me for your lover?
Madam answer Yes or No.'
'Oh No John, No John, No John No!'

'Madam let us walk your garden,
Walk and talk as lovers do;
Madam would you take it unkindly
If I picked a rose and pinned on you?'
'Oh No John, No John, No John No!'

'Madam if I fixed your garter
Just an inch above the knee
And if perchance my hand should wander
Would you think it rude of me?'
'Oh No John, No John, No John No!'

'Madam why not strip stark naked,
Go to bed as lovers do?

Madam would you be offended
If I undressed and came with you?'
'Oh No John, No John, No John No!'

'Now we are in bed together
Gazing on each other's charms;
Madam tell me would your husband
Please you better in your arms?'
'Oh No John, No John, No John No!'

'Madam rise, draw back the curtains,
The morning cock is crowing high!
Madam rise, draw back the curtains,
Open your arms and let me fly!'
'Oh No John, No John, No John No!'

83. O That I Durst

This poem, which has a metaphorical ingenuity almost worthy of Donne, was printed in the drollery *Sportive Wit* (1656).

O that I durst but thread your needle, lady,
There would I work till I had made a baby.
Or stop your floodgates, on condition I
Did at the jointer in the river lie.

O that I durst but shoot a gulf I know,
Or in the Lower Countries my seed sow,
Or plough the bottom of that Netherland
Until my plough did fall, and I not stand.

O that I durst but play at in-and-in.
If I were out, I would again begin;
Or fast-or-loose, I care not whether much.
Yet should I lose at both, my play is such.

O that I durst tread the grass that grows
About your river, where perfect nectar flows,
Or that my smaller current might distil
His moisture into yours, till yours it fill.

O that I durst monopolise a thing,
I mean that curious black-enamelled ring
Whose virtue's such in durance that it has
Worn out a world of stones that did surpass.
  Yet I care not; for all that I will venture,
  If you'll give leave, within your ring to enter.

84. Ocean Liner

The reference to Bevan, built up by the British press as the
great socialist bogeyman of the '50s, suggests a fairly recent
origin. It has been suggested to me that the poem was
collectively composed by passengers on a voyage from Britain
to Australia; this, and No. 100, establishes the ocean as an
elemental source of bawdy inspiration.

It was on an Ocean Liner
And the nights had been made finer
Than the Gods who rule our morals could have wished;
And they were much revolted
To see this had resulted
In some women being disastrously dished.
To the women thus afflicted
This could hardly be depicted
As a practical variety of joke,
For if the truth be all admitted
With so many men they'd flitted,
That no certain blame attached to any bloke.
First, singly they suffered
And kept themselves well buffered
With smiling face to hide their secret shame;
For no one wished another
To realise a lover
Had toted her a babe without a name.
Soon, in ways but known to women,
They discovered that their sinnin'
Had in effect on each one been the same,
And so they pooled their forces
Discussing which of several courses
Would be the best to shift the stigma and the shame.
They took baths exceeding hot
They took quinine quite a lot
But every trusted remedy proved vain,
They took to jumping off the table
Used stilboestrol when able—
All that happened was that they had a lot of pain.
Ergot and mercuric chloride

Kept them up nights tired and sore-eyed
As they waited, watched and looked for signs in vain.
Even remedies more drastic,
Such as knitting needles (plastic)
Failed to make these tortured girls themselves again.
The gods who rule our morals
With all this had no quarrels,
To them it was a proper punishment for sin.
When elections came in Heaven
And led by Aneurin Bevan,
The opposition Party had got in,
They removed the gods we mentioned
And put in a well intentioned
Really most efficient Commissar of Sex.
Birth Control was his forte
And though you think it naughty,
He taught little girls some ways the sperm to vex.
The world, it should be stated,
He thought over-populated,
And the technique of his predecessor nuts,
So when he saw these girls in trouble
He sent information at the double
To assist them with the problem of their guts.
Now his piece of information
Caused these girls some consternation,
For it stated, short and sweet, 'Just try some gin'.
Still, as other things had failed
And by now at nought they quailed
They took a bottle and a glass and pushed it in.
The results as you may guess
Were really quite a mess
And they suffered quite unmentionable pain,
But although it wrecked their tummies
It stopped them being mummies
So their drunken agony had not been in vain.
Since this heavenly defection
There has been a re-election,
The gods of morals once again in office rest,
But the trouble has been done
The information won
And to women gin remains for ever blessed.

85. Of All the Seas

A seventeenth-century poem from Percy's Folio MS (see headnote to No. 5); the ferret's penetrative powers have made it probably the most common of animal sexual symbols.

Of all the seas that's coming,
Of all the woods that's rising,
Of all the fishes in the sea,
Give me a woman's swiving.

For she hath pretty fancies
To pass away the night;
And she hath pretty pleasures
To conjure down a sprite.

My father gave me land,
My mother gave me money,
And I have spent it every whit
In hunting of a coney.

I hunted up a hill,
A coney did espy;
My ferret seeing that,
Into her hole did hie.

My ferret seeing that,
Into her hole did run;
But when he came into her hole,
No coney could be found.

I put it in again;
I found her out at last;
The coney then betwixt her legs
Did hold my ferret fast.

Till that it was so weak,
Alack it could not stand!
My ferret then out of her hole
Did come into my hand.

All you that be good fellows,
Give hearing unto me;
And if you would a coney hunt,
A black one let it be;

For black ones are they best,
Their skins will yield most money.
I would to God that he were hanged,
That does not love a coney.

86: Old Farmer

A cyclical use of teasing rhymes from the late Victorian period; tease-songs, as such, became popular during the eighteenth century.

There was an old farmer who sat on a rock,
Stroking his whiskers and shaking his
Fist at the children who wanted to pass;
So they gave him a turnip to stick up his
Trousers, which were worn out and falling apart,
Because he'd just let off a juicy great
Pigeon, which decided to join in the hunt,
Thinking he fancied a nice bit of
Shelter in the cow-shed from the rain and the squalls;
But a man with a gun came and shot off his
Mouth at a lady who walked like a duck,
And said she had found out a new way to
Educate the children to sew and to knit,
While the lads of the village were shovelling the
Muck and the manure in a state of great bliss,
Waiting for the farmer's wife to finish her
Song of the farmer who sat on a rock,
Stroking, &c.

87. On Monday

An early twentieth-century rhyme which depicts woman as a Venus flytrap out to catch man by the flies.

On Monday I touched her on the ankle
On Tuesday I touched her on the knee
On Wednesday with success
I lifted up her dress
On Thursday her chemise;
On Friday I put my hand upon it
Next day she gave my balls a tweak
And on Sunday after supper
I stuffed the bugger up her
And now I'm paying seven and six a week.

88. Once Twice Thrice

A broadside catch of 1695 in which the narrator is driven to drink through sexual despair.

Once, twice, thrice I Julia tried,
The scornful puss as oft denied,
And since, and since, I can no better, better thrive,
I'll cringe to ne'er a bitch alive,
So kiss my arse, so kiss my arse, so kiss my arse,
So kiss my arse disdainful sow,
Good claret, good claret is my mistress now.

89. O'Reilly

This song, from the last half of the nineteenth century, was kept gloriously alive by the servicemen of two world wars; the metamorphosis of pisspot (A-text) to pistol (B-text) may have been a result of creative mishearing.

A

As I was sitting by the fire
Smoking pipe and drinking porter
Suddenly the thought came into my head:
I'd like to fuck O'Reilly's daughter.
Diddy-I-ay, diddy-I-O
For the one-eyed Reilly,
Rub-a-dub-dub-dub, balls and all,
Hey-jig-a-jig, très bon.

I took that maiden up to bed,
Made her cross her left leg over;
Never a word that maiden said,
Snorted like hell when the fuck was over.
Diddy-I-ay, &c.

Sound of footsteps on the stair:
Up came O'Reilly breathing slaughter;
Bloody great pisspot in his hand
After the man who'd fucked his daughter.
Diddy-I-ay, &c.

I took him by the scruff of the neck,
Stuck his head in a bucket of water,
Stuffed the pisspot up his arse
A bloody sight quicker than I'd fucked his daughter.
Diddy-I-ay, &c.

B

As I was drinking in Reilly's bar
Getting pissed on gin and water
Suddenly a thought came into my head:

Why not fuck old Reilly's daughter?
Ee-eye-ee-eye-eye-ay
For the one-eyed Reilly;
Rub-a-dub and balls and all,
Ring-a-ling-a-ling, très bon.

I laid her gently on her bed
And quickly cocked my left leg over;
Not a word the maiden said
But laughed like hell till the job was over.
Ee-eye, &c.

I heard a footstep on the stair –
Who should it be but the one-eyed Reilly,
Bloody great pistol in his hand,
Looking for the man who'd screwed his daughter.
Ee-eye, &c.

I seized him by the hairs of his head
And stuffed his head in a bucket of water,
Rammed the pistol up his arse
Harder than I rammed his daughter.
Ee-eye. &c.

C
'Good morning, Mister Reilly,
Good morning to your soul;
I tried to fuck your daughter
But I couldn't find her hole.

At last I found her hole, Sir,
And tried it with my pin
And then, to tell the truth Sir,
I couldn't get it in.

At last I got it in, Sir,
And waggled it about
And then, to tell the truth Sir,
I couldn't get it out.

At last I got it out, Sir,
All red and sore
And I swear, dear Mister Reilly,
I'li fuck that girl no more.'

90. Origin of Copulation

From *The Pearl* (5 November 1879); it illustrates the magazine's editorial policy of treating the nymphomaniac as the ideal woman.

Success to Dame Nature for 'twas by her plan
That woman first thought of enjoyment from man;
She knew that of pleasure they'd never be sick
And so out of kindness invented a prick!
    A stiff standing glorious prick!
    Voluptuous, rubicund prick!
O surely of fortune it came in the nick,
Good-natured dame Nature to give us a prick!

Without it how lost would a poor maiden be,
It tickles her quim, makes her water run free;
Most women a handle would have to their front,
So they've only to thrust a long prick in their cunt!
    Their hairy voluptuous cunt!
    Their sweet little, queer little cunt!
What damsel no handle would have to her front?
And prick e'er has been a great friend unto cunt!

When nature to woman gave two mouths she willed,
Of course, that they both should be equally filled;
And if woman will look after one mouth, you know,
That prick will look after the mouth that's below!
    Stiff standing glorious prick!
    Voluptuous, rubicund prick!
O surely of fortune it came in the nick,
Good-natured dame Nature to give us a prick!

When sorrow torments lovely woman, O dear,
A mighty good fucking will banish despair;
If her belly but aches why we all know the trick,
There's nothing can ease it so well as a prick!
    A nice luscious prick!
    A stiff standing prick!
For any young maiden it can do the trick,
O joys there are plenty but nothing like prick!

91. Origin of Species

Darwin's *Origin of Species* (1859) banished Adam and Eve from the modern consciousness; this piece, which shows the titular influence of Darwin, appeared in *The Pearl* (1 July 1879) and provided a bawdy gloss on the authorised version of creation.

When Adam and Eve were first put into Eden,
They never once thought of that pleasant thing – breeding.
Though they had not a rag to cover their front
Adam sported his prick, and Eve sported her cunt.
        Derry down.

Adam's prick was so thick and so long – such a teaser;
Eve's cunt was so hairy and fat – such a breezer;
Adam's thing was just formed any maiden to please
And his bollocks hung down very near to his knees.
        Derry down.

Eve played with his balls, and thought it no harm,
He fingered her quim and ne'er felt alarm;
He tickled her bubbies she rubbed up his yard,
And yet for a fuck why they felt no regard.
        Derry down.

But when Mrs Eve did taste of the fruit
It was then that her eyes first beheld Adam's root;
Then he ate an apple, and after he had don't
Why then he first found out the value of cunt.
        Derry down.

Then they say they made fig leaves, that's fiddle-de-dee.
He wanted a quim, and quite ready was she;
They gazed on their privates with mutual delight,
And she soon found a hole to put jock out of sight!
        Derry down.

Then Adam soon laid Mrs Eve on the grass,
He popped in his prick, she heaved up her arse;

He wriggled, she wiggled, they both stuck to one tether
And she tickled his balls till they both came together!
                    Derry down.

Since then all her children are filled with desire,
And the women a stiff-standing prick all require,
And no son of Adam will e'er take affront
For where is the man that can live without cunt?
                    Derry down.

92. Our Gudewife's Sae Modest

Collected by Burns and printed in the *c.* 1800 *MMC*; the joke
at the expense of gentility is frequently echoed in Burns's own
poetry.

Our gudewife's sae modest,
   When she is set at meat,
A laverock's leg, or a tittling's wing,   *lark/sparrow*
   Is mair than she can eat;
But, when she's in her bed at e'en,
   Between me and the wa';
She is a glutton deevil,
   She swallows cocks an a'.

93. Our Lass Bess

Collected by Burns and printed in the *c.* 1800 *MMC*; the sexual nest-image should be compared to that in No. 31.

O ken ye na our lass, Bess?
An' ken ye na our lass, Bess?
Between her lily white thies
She's biggit a magpie's nest.

An' ken ye na our lad, Tam?
An' ken ye na our lad, Tam?
He's on o' a three-fitted stool,
An' up to the nest he clamb.

An' what did he there, think ye?
An' what did he there, think ye?
He brak a' the eggs o' the nest,
An' the white's ran down her thie.

94. Oyster Nan

From *Pills* where it is conspicuous for the absence of period poeticisms; the terminology ('lay', 'coming', &c.) is still remarkably fresh.

As Oyster Nan stood by her tub,
    To show her vicious inclination;
She gave her noblest parts a scrub,
    And sighed for want of copulation:
A vintner of no little fame,
    Who excellent red and white can sell ye,
Beheld the little dirty dame,
    As she stood scratching of her belly.

'Come in,' says he, 'you silly slut,
    'Tis now a rare convenient minute;
I'll lay the itching of your scut,
    Except some greedy devil be in it.'
With that the flat-capped fusby smiled,
    And would have blushed, but that she could not;
'Alas!' says she, 'we're soon beguiled,
    By men to do those things we should not.'

From door they went behind the bar,
    As it's by common fame reported;
And there upon a turkey chair,
    Unseen the loving couple sported:
But being called by company,
    As he was taking pains to please her;
'I'm coming, coming Sir,' says he,
    'My dear, and so am I,' says she, Sir.

Her molehill belly swelled about,
    Into a mountain quickly after;
And when the pretty mouse crept out,
    The creature caused a mighty laughter:
And now she has learned the pleasing game,
    Although much pain and shame it cost her;
She daily ventures at the same,
    And shuts and opens like an oyster.

95. Parson

A bawdy version of Child's traditional ballad 'Our Goodman' (274), this is still popular with the student fraternity.

Oh, the parson came home drunk,
As drunk as buggery,
He saw some shoes beside the bed
Where his shoes ought to be;
'Oh, my dear wife, my darling wife, my beautiful wife,' said he,
'What are those shoes beside the bed, where my shoes ought to be?'
'Oh, you old fool, you damn fool, you bloody great fool,' said she,
'It is that selfsame pisspot that you once gave to me.'
Oh, the parson said, 'Yo-ho, I've travelled the wide world o'er,
But a pisspot with laces in I never did see before.'

Oh, the parson came home drunk,
As drunk as buggery,
He saw a head in his wife's bed
Where his head ought to be;
'Oh, my dear wife, my darling wife, my beautiful wife,' said he,
'What is that head that's in the bed, where my head ought to be?'
'Oh, you old fool, you damn fool, you bloody great fool,' said she,
'It is that selfsame baby's arse that you once gave to me.'
Oh, the parson said, 'Yo-ho, I've travelled the wide world o'er,
But a baby's arse with whiskers on I never did see before.'

Oh, the parson came home drunk,
As drunk as buggery,
He saw a mess on his wife's dress
Where his mess ought to be;
'Oh, my dear wife, my darling wife, my beautiful wife,' said he,

'What is that mess that's on your dress, where my mess ought
        to be?'
'Oh, you old fool, you damn fool, you bloody great fool,' said
        she,
'It is that selfsame Nestle's milk that you once gave to me.'
Oh, the parson said, 'Yo-ho, I've travelled the wide world
        o'er,
But Nestle's milk that stinks of fish I never did see before.'

Oh, the parson came home drunk,
As drunk as buggery,
He saw a thing in his wife's thing
Where his thing ought to be;
'Oh, my dear wife, my darling wife, my beautiful wife,' said
        he,
'What is that thing that's in your thing, where my thing
        ought to be?'
'Oh, you old fool, you damn fool, you bloody great fool,' said
        she,
'It is that selfsame rolling pin that you once gave to me.'
Oh, the parson said, 'Yo-ho, I've travelled the wide world
        o'er,
But a rolling pin with ballocks on I never did see before.'

96. Pastoral

A stylistically contrived piece of bawdry recited at the Beggar's Benison club (see headnote to No. 2).

'Twas noon in the month of May,
And birds did sing on every brae;
'Neath a spreading tree, nigh Balcarres steep,
A maiden fair lay fast asleep.
Gentle zephyrs from the skies
Had blown the clothes up o'er her thighs;
And a youth, who'd sought the shade to rest
From behind a tree spied Cupid's nest.
But her legs were crossed – what could he do
Though heaven itself appeared in view? –
Till Cupid sent a little fly
Upon the maiden's lily-white thigh.
The maiden, thus tickled and void of care,
Threw one leg here and the other leg there.
The impassioned youth enraptured grew,
Love's 'rosy arrow' forth he drew,
And softly bending on his knees,
Gently he lifted her chemise,
Too late the maiden fair awoke,
Love's 'arrow' made her sigh each stroke;
Yet bleeding, panting with sweet pain,
She smiled and bade him try again.

97. Pillycock

In Shakespeare's time 'pillicock' was a common term for the penis; this poem from *Pills* gives the organ an objective and independent existence.

Pillycock came to my lady's toe
And there the whoreson began to go;
Had he feet, ay marry had he?
And did he go, ay marry did he?
    So bolt upright and ready to fight,
    And Pillycock he lay there all night.

Pillycock came to my lady's heel
And there the whoreson began to feel;
Had he hands, ay marry had he?
And did he feel, ay marry did he?
    So bolt, &c.

Pillycock came to my lady's shin
And there the whoreson began to grin;
Had he teeth, ay marry had he?
And did he grin, ay marry did he?
    So bolt, &c.

Pillycock came to my lady's knee
And there the whoreson began to see;
Had he eyes, ay marry had he?
And did he see, ay marry did he?
    So bolt, &c.

Pillycock came to my lady's thigh
And there the whoreson began to fly;
Had he wings, ay marry had he?
And did he fly, ay marry did he?
    So bolt, &c.

Pillycock came to my lady's cunt
And there the whoreson began to hunt;
Had he hounds, ay marry had he?

And did he hunt, ay marry did he?
  So bolt, &c.

Pillycock came to my lady's quilt
And there the whoreson began to tilt;
Had he lance, ay marry had he?
And did he tilt, ay marry did he?
  So bolt, &c.

98. Ploughman

The act of the ploughman penetrating the earth prior to the sowing of seed is an ancient sexual symbol; Burns modelled his song of the same name on this which was printed in the *c.* 1800 *MMC.*

The ploughman he's a bonnie lad,
  His mind is ever true, jo;
His garters knit below the knee,
  His bonnet it is blue, jo.
    Sing up wi't a', the ploughman lad,
    And hey the merry ploughman;
    O' a' the trades that I do ken,
    Commend me to the ploughman.

As wakin' forth upon a day
  I met a jolly ploughman,
I tald him I had lands to plough,
  If he wad prove true, man.
    Sing, &c.

He says 'My dear, take ye nae fear,
  I'll fit you till a hair, jo;
I'll cleave it up, and hit it down,
  And water-furrow't fair, jo.'
    Sing, &c.

'I hae three ousen in my plough,   *oxen*
  Three better ne'er ploughed ground, jo.
The foremost ox is lang and sma',
  The twa are plump and round, jo.'
    Sing, &c.

Then he wi' speed did yoke his plough,
  Which by a gaud was driven, jo!   *goad*
But when he wan between the stilts
  I thought I was in heaven, jo!
    Sing, &c.

But the foremost ox fell in the fur,
    The tither twa did founder;
The ploughman lad he breathless grew,
    In faith it was nae wonder.
    Sing, &c.

But a sykie risk, below the hill,   *watery marsh*
    The plough she took a stane, jo,
Which gart the fire flee frae the sock,   *ploughshare*
    The ploughman gied a grane, jo.   *groan*
    Sing, &c.

'I hae ploughed east, I hae ploughed west,
    In weather foul and fair, jo;
But the sairest ploughing e'er I ploughed
    Was ploughing amang hair, jo.'
    Sing, &c.

99. Poor Little Angeline

Enjoyed by the servicemen of World War Two and twentieth century in origin, it has the advantage of a simple refrain that positively demands audience participation.

She was sweet sixteen, little Angeline,
Pure and simple as the village green.
A virgin still, never had a thrill,
   Poor little Angeline.

Now the village squire had a low desire
To be the filthiest bugger in the whole damn shire
And he's set his heart on a vital part of
   Poor little Angeline.

At the village fair the squire was there
Masturbating in the village square
When he chanced to see the dainty knee of
   Poor little Angeline.

As she lifted her skirt to avoid the dirt
She stepped between the puddles of the squire's last spurt
And his tool peeled raw at the sight he saw of
   Poor little Angeline

So he lifted his hat and he said, 'Your cat
Has been run over and is squashed right flat;
My car's in the square, may I drive you there
   Poor little Angeline?'

Now this lowdown turd deserved the bird,
But Angeline she followed him without a word.
As they drove away you could hear the people say
   'Poor little Angeline.'

Now they hadn't gone far when he stopped the car,
Dragged Angeline into a nearby bar;
Filled her up with gin, just to tempt her into sin –
   Poor little Angeline.

Then he took her to a dell which he knew very well,
Started giving Angeline bloody fucking hell
As he tried his luck in a lowdown fuck with
  Poor little Angeline.

If the truth be told, the blacksmith bold
Had loved little Angeline for years untold
And she loved him too and had promised to be true –
  Poor little Angeline.

But sad to say, this very day
The blacksmith had been thrown in gaol in this very way
For coming in his pants at the local dance with
  Poor little Angeline.

Now the window of his cell overlooked the very dell
Where the squire was giving Angeline bloody fucking hell
And down amongst the grass he recognised the arse of
  Poor little Angeline.

Then he gave a mighty start and he blew a mighty fart,
Blasted the prison walls right apart,
Then he ran like shit lest the squire should split
  Poor little Angeline.

When he got to the spot and he saw what was what
He tied the squire's chopper in a bloody great knot!
As he lay on his guts he got a kick in the nuts from
  Poor little Angeline.

'Oh blacksmith true! I love you, I do!
And I see by your trousers that you love me too!
As I'm all undressed you may do your best on
  Poor little Angeline.'

Now the rest of my song won't take very long
Since the blacksmith had a pecker that was one foot long
And this man's charm was as strong as his right arm.
  Poor little Angeline!

100. Portion of a Woman

Once a poem passes into oral circulation it becomes public property and is subject to the changes associated with frequent transmission. This, however, has preserved its rhythmic shape pretty consistently for half a century. According to his autobiography, *A.P.H. His Life and Times* (London 1970, pp. 65–7) Sir Alan Herbert originally composed this celebrated piece in *c.* 1928 on a voyage from Ceylon to Britain. Passing through the Red Sea, Sir Alan consulted the ship's doctor and, while waiting for attention, 'dipped into some of his learned books. There was one which seemed to be the medical version of What Every Married Man Ought to Know. I had been married for nearly twenty-five years, and was amazed to find how little I knew about the female form divine.' The book was borrowed, the climate was excruciatingly hot so – as a diversion – Sir Alan wrote 'Lines on a Book Borrowed from the Ship's Doctor'. The poem was presented to the purser and 'From these beginnings the damned composition went, first all round London, and then all round the world . . . I have a shrewd fear that if any of my works survive me long it will be this blasted work.' The authentic version is given on p. 65 of Sir Alan's autobiography.

A

The portions of a woman which appeal to man's depravity
Are constructed with considerable care;
What would seem at first a simple little cavity
Is really an elaborate affair.

Now doctors of distinction who have studied this phenomenon
In a number of experimental dames
Have made a list of all their feminine abdomina
And given them delightful Latin names.

There's the vulva, the vagina, and the jolly old perineum
And the hymen (sometimes found in brides)
And lots of other gadgets which you'd love if you could see
     them:
The clitoris and lord knows what besides.

Now isn't it a pity that we in common chatter
Re this mystery for which men often hunt
Must use for all this complicated matter
Such a brief and unattractive word as cunt.

B

Those portions of a female which appeal to man's depravity
Are constructed with considerable care,
And what at first appears to be a simple little cavity
Is really an elaborate affair.

Now Doctors of distinction have examined these phenomena
On numbers of experimental dames,
And classified the organs of the feminine abdomina
And given them delightful Latin names:

There's the vulva, the vagina, and the jolly old perineum,
And the hymen in the case of many brides;
There are many other things that you would love if you could
    see 'em.
The clitoris and lots of things besides.

So isn't it a pity when we common people chatter
Of the mysteries to which I have referred,
We should use for such a delicate and complicated matter
Such a short and unattractive little word.

C

The portions of a woman that appeal to man's depravity
Are constructed with considerable care,
And what at first appears to be a simple little cavity
Is really a most intricate affair!

There's the vulva, the vagina and the jolly perineum
And the hymen – which is sometimes found in brides –
Plus scores of other gadgets which would please if we could
    see 'em
Like the clitoris and God knows what besides.

So isn't it a pity that when common people chatter
Of the mysteries to which I have referred

They should have for such a delicate and intricate a matter
Such a very short and inartistic word!

D

That portion of a woman that appeals to man's depravity
Is constructed with extraordinary care,
And what is apt to be known as a little cavity
Is really an elaborate affair.

There's the clitoris, the vagina, the jolly perineum,
The hymen found in quite a lot of brides,
And many other gadgets you would find if you could see
    'em –
The uterus and many more besides.

What a pity it is when we common people chatter
Of the thing to which I have referred
That we call such a delicate and complicated matter
By such a very short and very vulgar word.

101. Pudding

From *Pills*; it gives a gastronomical gloss to a sexual encounter in which, as is usual in bawdry, the female proves most durable.

From twelve years' old I oft have been told
A pudding it was a delicate bit;
I can remember my mother has said
What a delight she had to be fed
    With a pudding.

Thirteen being past I longed for to taste
What nature or art could make it so sweet;
For many gay lassies about my age
Perpetually speak on't, that puts me in a rage
    For a pudding.

Now at fifteen I often have seen
Most maids to admire it so;
That their humour and pride is to say
O what a delight they have for to play
    With a pudding.

When I am among some wives that are young
Who think they shall never give it due praise;
'It is sweet, it is good, it is pleasant still,'
They cry, they think they shall ne'er have their fill
    Of a pudding.

The greater sort of the town and the court,
When met, their tongues being tippled with wine;
How merry and jocund their tattles do run
To tell how they ended and how they begun
    With a pudding.

Some ancient wives who most of their lives
Have daily tasted of the like food
Now for want of supplies do swear and grumble
That still they're able enough to mumble
    A pudding.

Now now I find, cat will to kind,
Since all my heart and blood is on fire,
I am resolved whatever comes on't
My fancy no longer shall suffer the want
              Of a pudding.

For I'll to John who says he has one
That's crammed as close as a cracker or squib;
Who ever is telling me when we do meet
Of the wishing desires and sweetness they get
              In a pudding.

I thought at first it never would burst,
It was as hard as gristle or bone;
But by the rowling and trowling about
How kindly and sweetly the marrow flew out
              Of his pudding.

Well, since I ne'er was fed with such gear
Until my John did prove so kind
I made a request to prepare again
That I might continue in love with the strain
              Of his pudding.

Then straight he brought what I little thought
Could ever have been in its former plight;
He rumbled and jumbled me o'er and o'er,
Till I found he had almost wasted the store
              Of his pudding.

Then the other mess I begged him to dress
Which by my assistance was brought to pass;
But by his dullness and moving so slow
I quickly perceived the stuffing grew low
              In his pudding.

Though he grew cold my stomach did hold
With vigour to relish the other bit;
But all he could do could not furnish again
For he swore he had left little more than the skin
              Of his pudding.

102. Put It In

An eighteenth-century broadside that mercifully refrains from a heavy moralistic finale.

A country lad and bonny lass they did together meet
And as they did together pass thus he began to greet!
'What I do say I may mind well, and thus I do begin:
If you would have your belly swell hold up, and I'll put in.'

'O Sir,' quoth she, 'I love the sport, yet am afraid to try,
And for your love, I thank you for't, find but conveniency;
My mind I'll tell you by and by, your love my heart doth
    win,
And presently I down will lie, O then boy push it in.'

He clasped this damsel round the waist and softly laid her
    down,
Yea wantonly he her embraced and her delights did crown;
'Thrust home', quoth she, 'my brisk young lad, 'tis but a
    venial sin,
For I should soon have run quite mad had you not put it in.'

The sport he did so close pursue that he was quickly tired,
And when he did her beauty view his heart again was fired;
He came on with such fresh supplies he did her favour win,
And finding babies in her eyes he bravely thrust it in.

'What pleasure is there like to this,' this damsel then did cry,
'I've heard them talk of lovers' bliss, O what a fool was I
So long to live a maid ere I did this same sport begin;
This death I now could freely die, I prithee thrust it in.'

She held this youngster to his task till he began to blow;
Then at the last he leave did ask and so she let him go.
Then down he panting lay awhile and rousing up again
She charmed him with a lovely smile again to put it in.

To work he went most earnestly her fancy to fulfil,
Till at the last she loud did cry 'I do't with such good will,

188

I pleasure feel in every vein, my joys do now begin,
O dearest quickly to't again and stoutly thrust it in.'

She seemed at last to be content and glad at heart was he,
His youthful strength was almost spent, so brisk a lass was she;
He vowed he never was so matched nor ne'er shall be again,
And for that time they both dispatched though he had put it
    in.

But when she from him parted was thus she began to cry,
'Was ever any wanton lass in such a case as I?
He that hath got my maidenhead I ne'er shall see again,
And now my heart is almost dead to think he put it in.

But yet it had the sweetest taste that ever mortal knew,
Our time we did not vainly waste, believe me this is true;
Should I e'er see my bonny lad I'd venture once again,
And let the world account me mad, again I'll put it in.'

103. Queen and Louise

A common impulse of the bawdy muse is to pull down pomposity and a prime target is the aristocracy. Victoria's daughter Louise married John Campbell, Marquis of Lorne, on 21 March 1871. The event prompted this entirely apocryphal dialogue between mother and daughter and it has had an underground existence to the present day.

The Queen and Louise sat down to their teas
And spoke in a manner forlorn,
For in less than a week Louisa the freak
Was to marry the Marquis of Lorne.

Said the Queen, 'Now, my dear, your marriage draws near,
Your great day of confetti and rice,
So I feel that I should – as I promised I would –
Deliver some fucking advice!

Now Lorne comes of a stock that's renowned for its cock
And I don't think that he is a noodle;
At the sight of his prick don't pretend to be sick
But just give him plenty of doodle.

On that very first night you should moan with delight
As his hand wanders over your belly.
You may whimper a bit, but on no account shit
Though he mangles your tits to a jelly!

Once his prick's in your quim, though the work's up to him
Keep the cheeks of your arse gently wagging;
To the beat of his prick keep time to a tick
For therein lies the beauty of shagging!'

The Princess Louise went down on her knees
As naked as when she was born:
With a hand on her twat she said, 'Just look at that –
It was made for the Marquis of Lorne.'

104. Rangy Lil

Still orally alive, a version of this tale of sexual combat appeared in *Immortalia*, New York 1927, but, like 'Eskimo Nell', it was probably composed under the influence of Service's *Songs of a Sourdough* (1907) – see headnote to No. 39. Legman (pp. 418–20) traces the theme back to the seventeenth century and claims that 'Eskimo Nell' is 'a British imitation' of Lil. If that is the case the imitator effortlessly improved on the original.

Don't move away there, stranger!
That ain't shit upon the seat;
I've just come back from the north country
And the mud's still on my feet.

I reckon you never heard tell
Of a whore called Rangy Lil
Or the fate that overtook her
Back of the shithouse on Dougan's Hill.

Now Rangy Lil was a schoolmarm
When first she came out west,
But she gave up teachin' for fuckin'
'Cos she liked fuckin' best.

And when she fucked she fucked for keeps,
She piled her victims up in heaps.

There was a standing bet in our home town
That no young man could fuck Lil down,

Till over the hill from Dragarse Creek
Came a short-shit fucker called One-ball Pete.

He laid his tool on Murphy's bar
And I swear it stretched from thar-to-thar.

A contest was fixed twixt him and Lil
Back of the shithouse on Dougan's Hill.

Where every man could find a seat
And watch that greaser sink his meat.

The contest began with grace and ease
With the wind moaning through the sycamore trees.

Now Lil had shunts and double shunts
And tricks unknown to common cunts,

But the half-breed was up to every trick,
He just kept reeling out more prick.

Then – in the middle of her stroke –
He turned and nailed her as she broke!

And through the portals of Lil's ass
A foot of jet-black penis passed,

And folk drove up for miles around
To see where Lil's ass tore up the ground,

But they nailed her pants to the shithouse door
In memory of a plucky whore – Rangy Lil.

105. Red Flag

This parody of the Labour Party's favourite conference-song is probably of student origin.

'Twas on a warm and sultry day
As on a bank a maiden lay;
And as she lay in sweet repose
A breath of wind blew up her clothes.
A sailor who was passing by
He smiled a smile and winked his eye
But then he saw to his despair
She had the red flag flying there!

The working class may kiss my arse,
I have the foreman's job at last!
Not only in the summer time
But when the world is white with rime:
The working class may kiss my arse
I have the foreman's job at last.

106. Reels o' Bogie

Collected by Burns and printed in the '1827' *MMC*; the notion of dancing as a surrogate for sex is here made explicit.

You lads and lasses all that dwell
   In the town of Strathbogie,
Whene'er you meet a pretty lass,
   Be sure you tip her cogie.   *wooden pail*
The lads and lasses toy and kiss,
   The lads ne'er think it is amiss
To bang the holes whereout they piss,
   And that's the reels o' Bogie.

There's Kent, and Keen, and Aberdeen,
   And the town of Strathbogie,
Where every lad may have his lass,
   Now that I've got my cogie.
They spread wide their snow-white thighs
   And roll about their wanton eyes,
And when they see your pintle rise
   They'll dance the reels o' Bogie.

A trooper going o'er the lea,
   He swore that he would steer me,
And long before the break of day,
   He giggled, goggled near me.
He put a stiff thing in my hand,
   I could not bear the banging o't
But long before he went away
   I suppled both the ends o't.

His pintle was of largest size,
   Indeed it was a banger,
He sought a prize between my thighs
   Till it became a hanger.
Had you but seen the wee bit skin
   He had to put his pintle in,
You'd sworn it was a chitterling   *shirt frill*
   Dancing the reels o' Bogie.

He turned about to fire again
   And give me t'other sally,
And as he fired I ne'er retired
   But received him in my alley.
His pebbles they went thump, thump,
   Against my little wanton rump,
But soon I left him but the stump
   To dance the reels o' Bogie.

Said I, 'Young man, more you can't do,
   I think I've granted your desire,
By bobbing on my wanton clue,   *narrow glen*
   You see your pintle's all on fire.
When on my back I work like steel
   And bar the door with my left heel,
The more you fuck the less I feel,
   And that's the reels o' Bogie.'

107. Ringerangeroo

Of twentieth-century origin and still orally active.

A Ringerangeroo –
And what is that?
It's something soft
Like a pussy cat:
It's covered with hair
And split in two,
That's what they call
A Ringerangeroo.

108. Roger

From *Pills*; an early verbal portrait of the familiar lecher.

O mother, Roger with his kisses
    Almost stops my breath, I vow;
Why does he gripe my hand to pieces,
    And yet he says he loves me too?
    Tell me, mother, pray now do!
    Pray now do, pray now, do,
    Pray now, pray now, pray now do,
    What Roger means when he does so?
    For never stir I long to know.

Nay more, the naughty man beside it,
    Something in my mouth he put;
I called him beast and tried to bite it
    But for my life I cannot do't.
    Tell me, &c.

He sets me in his lap whole hours
    Where I feel I know not what;
Something I never felt in yours,
    Pray tell me, mother, what is that?
    Tell me, &c.

109. Sailor

A late Victorian mini-saga of sexual betrayal.

One day a year ago a sailor came to me
Looking for a lodging before he went to sea;
I being foolish thought it no harm
Jumped in beside him just to keep him warm.
And in the morning when he awoke
He put his hand in his pocket and pulled out a note.
'Take this,' he said, 'for what I have done
And holy Jesus Christ grant it be a son,
If it be a daughter bounce her on your knee,
If it be a son send the bastard out to sea;
A pair of bell-mouthed trousers
And a suit of navy-blue,
Let him climb the rigging as I've just climbed you.'
Now you young ladies take a warning from me,
Never let a sailor one inch above your knee.
I trusted one and see what he has done,
I've a pair of dirty bastards to dance upon my knee.

110. Sailor's Farewell

A crude twentieth-century descendant of the 'last farewells' of traditional ballads and broadsides.

May itching piles consume you
With syph and clap complete,
And lice as large as lobsters
Into your ballbag eat.

And when you're fucked and buggered
Like some old tossed off wreck
May you fall, inside out, through your arsehole
And break your bastard neck!

111. Samuel Hall

Jack Hall, a chimney sweep, was hanged in London in 1701 for burglary; as was customary the broadside writers issued his lamentable 'last goodnight' before the actual execution. As the printed words passed into the oral tradition the hapless Jack Hall was metamorphosed to the defiant Samuel Hall whose cry of 'Damn your eyes' is perennially popular.

O my name is Samuel Hall, Samuel Hall,
O my name is Samuel Hall, Samuel Hall,
   O my name is Samuel Hall
   And I've only got one ball
But that's better than fuck all
   Damn your eyes, blast your soul,
   Bloody hell, two-three-four,
   SHIT!

O they say I killed a man, killed a man,
O they say I killed a man, killed a man,
   O I hit him on the head
   With a bloody great lump of lead
Now the silly bastard's dead
   Damn, &c.

O they say I've got to swing, got to swing,
O they say I've got to swing, got to swing,
   O they say I've got to swing
   On a bloody great hunk of string
What a fucking awful thing
   Damn, &c.

O the sheriff he will come, he will come,
O the sheriff he will come, he will come,
   O the sheriff he will come
   With his gallows up his bum
He can stuff those gallows, chum,
   Damn, &c.

O the preacher he'll be there, he'll be there,
O the preacher he'll be there, he'll be there,

O the preacher he'll be there
And he'll offer up a prayer
Though I couldn't fucking care
Damn, &c.

O they say I'll go to hell, go to hell,
O they say I'll go to hell, go to hell,
O they say I'll go to hell
'Cos the preacher he can tell
He must know the bastard well
Damn, &c.

O and now I'm down in hell, down in hell,
O and now I'm down in hell, down in hell,
O and now I'm down in hell
And there's a bloody awful smell
'Cos the preacher's here as well
Damn, &c.

112. She Had to Go and Lose It

If beauty is in the eye of the beholder then obscenity is in the mind of the ogler; this twentieth-century poem derives its erotic impact entirely by suggestion.

We'd like to tell you a little story about a young girl about eighteen years old, about five-feet-two tall, and about to go out. Now her mother, realising it was her first time out with a young man, took her into the bedroom and said: 'Now Minnie, you're all dressed up in your finery, your very best clothes, and you look beautiful, you look gorgeous, you're alluring; and now, Minnie, I want you to remember everything I've ever told you and above all to be VERY VERY CAREFUL.'

But she had to go and lose it at the Astor,
She didn't take her mother's good advice;
After all there aren't so many girls who have one
And she'd never let it go for any price.

But she had to go and lose it at the Astor,
She didn't know exactly who to blame;
And she couldn't say just how or when she lost it,
She only knew she had it when she came.

They questioned all the bellboys and the porter,
The chef appeared to be the guilty guy
And the doorman also acted quite suspicious
But he coyly said, 'I'm sure it wasn't I.'

They searched the place from penthouse to the cellar,
In every room and underneath each bed;
Once they thought they saw it lying on a pillow
But they found it belonged to someone else instead.

And just as they were giving up their searching
The chauffeur walked up with it in his hand;
All they did was stand and gape –
There was Minnie's sable cape
AND SHE THOUGHT THAT SHE HAD LOST IT AT
    THE ASTOR.

113. She Wears

A song understandably attractive to the sexually under-privileged servicemen of World War Two.

She wears her silk pyjamas in summer when it's hot,
She wears her flannel nightie in winter when it's not,
But sometimes in the springtime and sometimes in the fall
She creeps between the bedclothes with fuck all on at all.

So glory, glory, glory, to summer when it's hot,
And glory, glory, glory, to winter when it's not,
But *Gloria in Excelsis* to springtime and the fall
When she creeps between the bedclothes with fuck all on at
    all.

114. She Wore No Blouse

A cautionary tale frequently sung – to the tune of 'She Wore a Tulip' – during World War Two and perhaps inspired by the extramural activities of the troops.

She wore no blouse and I wore no trousers,
We wore no underclothes;
When she caressed me she bloody near undressed me,
It's a thrill that no one knows.
I went to the doctor
Confessed that I had knocked her
Down where the green grass grows.
He said, 'My boy, the pimple
On the end of your winkle
Will grow just like a red, red rose.'

115. Susanna

One of the best bawdy poems to rely on teasing rhymes, it has gone the rounds for half a century.

Susanna was a lady with plenty of class
Who knocked 'em all dead when she wiggled her
 Eyes at the fellows as girls sometimes do
 To make it quite plain that she's aching to
Take in a movie or go for a sail
And then hurry home for a nice piece of
 Chocolate cake and a slice of roast duck
 For after a meal she was ready to
Go for a ride or a stroll on the dock
With any young man with a sizeable
 Roll of big bills and a pretty good front
 And if he talked fast she would show him her
Little pet dog which was subject to fits
And maybe she'd let him take hold of her
 Lilywhite hands with a movement so quick
 And then she'd reach over and tickle his
Chin while she showed him a trick learned in France
And ask the poor fellow to take off his
 Coat while she sang of the Indian shore
 For whatever she was Susanna was no bore.

116. Tailor

A seventeenth-century broadside which ridicules the tailor for having neither the quantity nor quality to satisfy his amorous customer.

In harvest-time I walked
   Hard by a corn-close side;
I hearing people talk,
   I looked about, and spied

A young man and a maid,
   Together they did lie;
When you hear it told
   You'll laugh full heartily.

She was as buxom a lass
   As any in our town;
She will not let you pass,
   But she'll call you to sit down.

A tailor passing by,
   She hit him on the heel:
'You are very welcome, Sir,
   To sit you down and feel.

What money's in my purse,
   At your command shall be,
If you will go along
   To Marson wake with me.'

He hearing her say so,
   And seeing her to smile,
Was charmed with her, so
   He sate him down a while.

And having groped her purse,
   And taken all her money,
He groped again, and missed,
   And caught her by the coney.

206

'Where am I now?' quoth he,
  'Another I have found;
It's not the same', quoth he,
  'For this is tufted round.'

'If it be tufted round,' quoth she,
  'There is good reason for't;
Therein such treasure lies
  Will make a tailor sport.'

He hearing her say so,
  Being a frolicsome lad,
Was willing for to know
  More of the fringed bag.

With that he eagerly
  To feel put forth his hand;
'Nay, hold good Sir,' said she,
  'Go not before you stand.

Except you take your yard,
  The depth of it to measure,
You'll find the purse so deep,
You'll hardly come to th'treasure.'

He hearing her say so,
  It put him to a stand;
She seeing him dismayed,
  She took his yard in hand:

'Is this your yard,' quoth she,
  'Is this your tailor's measure?
It is too short for me,
  It is not standard-measure.'

The tailor being abashed,
  She told him that it was
More fitter for a man
  Than such a penny ass.

She bids him now be gone,
  Since he could make no sport,

And said, 'Thou are too dull
  To enter such a fort.'

She looking fiercely at him,
  She said, 'Thou sneaking fool,
Go straight away to Vulcan
  And let him mend thy tool:

And tell him that Dame Venus
  At him is almost mad,
For sending to her school
  Such an unfit lad.'

You tailors that attempt
  Fringed bags to measure,
Be sure your yards be sealed,
  And of full standard-measure.

117. Taking a Maidenhead

From *The Pearl* (4 October 1879) whose credo it neatly summarises.

O maidenhead taking's a very great bore,
It makes cunt and prick so confoundedly sore;
But fucking the third time's like heaven above,
For your prick then glides in, as you draw on a glove!
  Gee up, Roger,
  Wag up, Roger,
  Roger's a thing that all women admire!

O give me a damsel of blooming fifteen,
With two luscious thighs and a mousetrap between,
With the fringe on the edge, and two red lips I say,
In her cunt I'd be diving by night and by day!
  Gee up, &c.

That woman would be a disgrace to our land,
Who would not take a prick when it stiffly does stand;
And when it droops low as if it were in dread,
She must tickle the balls, till it lifts up its head!
  Gee up, &c.

Cunt is a treasure which monarchs admire,
Cunt is a thing that my theme doth inspire;
Cunt is a mighty temptation to sin,
But cunt is a hole that I'd never be in!
  Gee up, &c.

Prick is its friend, its first cousin I ween,
Though prick I confess is a rare go-between;
Prick to a woman much joy can impart,
And prick is a thing that she loves in her heart!
  Gee up, &c.

Then here's to the female who yields to a man,
And here's to the man who'll fuck when he can,

For fucking creates all our joy upon earth,
And from fucking we know we all date our birth.
   Gee up, &c.

118. Tenement to Let

From *Pills*; shifts the favourite rural image of woman-as-luscious-landscape to the less imaginative domestic notion of woman-as-desirable-home.

I have a tenement to let,
   I hope will please you all;
And if you know the name of it
   'Tis called Cunny Hall.

It's seated in a pleasant vale
   Beneath a rising hill,
This tenement is to be let
   To whosoe'er I will.

For years, for months, for weeks, or days
   I'll let this famous bower;
Nay, rather than a tenant want
   I'd let it for an hour.

There's round about a pleasant grove
   To shade it from the sun,
And underneath is well water
   That pleasantly does run.

Where if you're hot you may be cooled,
   If cold you may find heat;
It is a well contrived spring,
   Not little nor too great.

The place is very dark by night
   And so it is by day;
But when you once are entered in
   You cannot lose your way.

And when you're in, go boldly on,
   As far as e'er you can;
And if you reach to the house top
   You'll be where ne'er was man.

119. These Foolish Things

The cynical resignation of this parody – of the song of the same name by Marvell, Strachey and Link – suggests the blacked-out mood of London during World War Two.

A

A wanky hanky in a London taxi,
Rude noises coming from a horse's jacksy,
The night that you had twins,
These foolish things
Remind me of you!

That rusty bedstead we had our first shags on,
The week of silence when you had the rags on,
Three weeks of creaking springs
These foolish things
Remind me of you.

A tattered fragment of a torn French Letter,
A hard red pimple that just won't get better,
How penicillin stings!
These foolish things
Remind me of you.

B

The sweaty sock beside the used French Letter,
The raging syphilis that won't get better,
O how the needle stings,
These foolish things
Remind me of you.

The night you caught your nipples in my braces,
My left-hand testicle that bears lipstick traces,
O how the needle stings,
These foolish things
Remind me of you.

120. This is His Life

The lament over impotence has a respectable literary pedigree (see headnote to No. 77); this – sung to the tune of 'The Church's One Foundation' – is a popular twentieth-century (*c.* 1920) account of the age-old problem.

A

From twenty to thirty if a man lives right
It is once in the morning and twice at night;
From thirty to forty if he still lives right
He misses a morning and sometimes a night;
From forty to fifty it is now and then;
From fifty to sixty it is God knows when;
From sixty to seventy if he is still inclined;
But don't let him kid you, it is still in his mind.
His sporting days are over,
His little light is out,
What used to be his sex appeal
Is now his water spout.
It used to be embarrassing
To make the thing behave
For nearly every morning
It stood and watched him shave.
But now it's getting older
It sure gives him the blues
To have it dangling down his legs
And watch him clean his shoes.

B

My days of youth are over
    My torch of life is out;
What used to be my sex appeal
    Is now my water spout.

Time was when of its own accord
    'Twould from my trousers spring
But now I've got a full time job
    To find the bloody thing.

It really was embarrassing
　The way it would behave
For early in the morning
　It would stand and watch me shave.

But as old age comes creeping on
　It sure gives me the blues
To see it hang its withered head
　And watch me clean my shoes.

C

My sporting days are over,
My pilot light is out,
What used to be my pecker
Is now my waterspout;
At twenty I was struggling
To make the brute behave
But stiffly every morning
It stood and watched me shave.

At thirty and at forty
I had some more control,
But sometimes it was naughty
As in the days of old;
But now I'm over fifty
And it gives me the blues
To see it hang there limply
And watch me shine my shoes.

D

Your spooning days are over,
Your pilot light is out,
What used to be your chopper
Is now your waterspout.
You used to be embarrassed
To make the brute behave
But every bloody morning
It stood and watched you shave.

214

At thirty and at forty
It kept itself afloat,
And stuck out horizontal
As you put on your coat.
But now you're well past forty
It sure gives you the blues,
To feel it hanging limply
And watch you shine your shoes.

121. Thrashing Machine

In 1786 Andrew Meikle designed the first really popular threshing machine; as it transformed the agricultural ritual in the nineteenth century so it was absorbed into the sexual folklore of the country.

For there was an old farmer in Down he did dwell,
He'd one pretty servant, her name it was Nell.
He'd one pretty servant she was scarce seventeen,
And he showed her the works of his thrashing machine.

Says Nell to the farmer, 'It's a fine summer's day,
While the rest of the farmers are off making hay,
Come into the barn where we won't be seen,
And the two of us start working our thrashing machine.'

Oh, Nell she stepped forward and into the house.
The boss got the harness and strapped her right on.
Nell took the handle and turned on the steam,
And the two of them start working their thrashing machine.

Oh, six months being over and nine coming on,
Nell's skirt wouldn't meet nor her drawers wouldn't go on;
It's under her oxter like a young fairy queen.
'I will have you transported for your thrashing machine.'

Oh, up comes the Judge with a pen in his claw,
He says, 'Lovely Nell, you have broken the law.'
'No, sir,' says she, 'it's plain to be seen,
I needed the strength of his thrashing machine.'

122. Tinker

Of all the sexual figures that haunt erotic folklore the most potent is the tinker, to whom there are many poetic tributes. Child's great romantic ballad 'The Gypsy Laddie' (200) presented a Heathcliff-like creature of pure passion but the more explicit acts of the tinker have been an essential part of oral poetry for centuries. In the course of time the puns on the tinker's near-magical ability to mend holes gave way to sheer sexual extravagance. The A-text is from *Choyce Drollery* (1656); the three following texts are traditional, B and C representing the living version of the subject.

A

He that a tinker, a tinker, a tinker will be,
Let him leave other loves, and come follow me.
Though he travels all the day,
Yet he comes home still at night,
And dallies, dallies with his doxy,
And dreams of delight.
His pot and his toast in the morning he takes,
And all the day long good music he makes;
He wanders up and down to wakes and to fairs,
He casts his cap, and casts his cap at the court and its cares;
And when to town the tinker doth come,
Oh, how the wanton wenches run,
Some bring him basins, and some bring him bowls,
All maids desire him to stop up their holes,
Prinkum Prankum is a fine dance, strong ale is good in the
     winter,
And he that thrums a wench upon a brass pot,
The child may prove a tinker.
With tink goes the hammer, the skellit and the scummer.
Come bring me thy copper kettle,
For the tinker, the tinker, the merry merry tinker
Oh, he's the man of mettle.

B

As I went down a shady lane at a door I chanced to knock,
The servant she came to the door and axed me could I stop,
Or could I mend a rusty hole that never had a drop?
Well, indeed I can, don't you know I can,
To me right-fol-looral-laddy, well indeed I can.

She brought me through the kitchen and she brought me
    through the hall,
And the servants cried: 'The devil, are you going to block us
    all?'
Well, indeed I'm not, don't you know I'm not,
To me right-fol-looral-laddy, well indeed I'm not.

She brought me up the stairs for to show me what to do.
She fell on the feather bed and I fell on it, too,
Well, indeed I did, don't you know I did,
To me right-fol-looral-laddy, well indeed I did.

She took up the frying pan and she began to knock,
O then for to let the servants know that I was at me work,
Well, indeed I was, you know I was,
To me right-fol-looral-laddy, well indeed I was.

She put her hand into her pocket and she pulled out fifty
    pound,
Sayin', 'Take this, me jolly tinker, and we'll have another
    round.'
Well, indeed I will, don't you know I will,
To me right-fol-looral-laddy, well indeed I will.

She put her hand into her pocket and she pulled out her gold
    watch,
Saying, 'Take this, me jolly tinker, for I know you are no
    botch.'
Well, indeed I'm not, don't you know I'm not,
To me right-fol-looral-laddy, well indeed I'm not.

Now I'm a jolly tinker this forty years or more,
And such a rusty hole as that I never blocked before.
Well, indeed I didn't, don't you know I didn't,
To me right-fol-looral-laddy, well indeed I didn't.

C

Oh once there was a tinker
As some folk used to say
And he used to ride a charger
Round the country every day
With his bloody great kidney wiper
And balls as big as three
And a yard and a half of foreskin
Hanging down below his knee;
Hanging down inches thick,
Hanging low – what a prick!
With a yard and a half of foreskin
Hanging down below his knee.

My Lady was a-dressing,
A-dressing for a Ball,
When she spied that dirty old tinker
Pissing up against her wall
With his bloody great, &c.

She wrote to him a letter
And in it she did say
She would rather be fucked by him, Sir,
Than her husband any day
With his bloody great, &c.

The tinker got that letter
And he began to read,
Then his balls began to fester
And his prick began to bleed
Yes his bloody great, &c.

He rode up to her mansion,
He rode up to her hall,
'Gor blimey,' said the butler,
'For he's come to fuck us all!
With his bloody great, &c.

He fucked them in the kitchen,
He fucked them in the hall,
But his buggering of that butler

Was his greatest feat of all
    With his bloody great, &c.

For first he fucked the housemaids
And then he fucked the wife
And then he fucked his charger
And ruined it for life
    With his bloody great, &c.

They say that tinker's dead, Sir,
They say he's gone to hell;
They say he fucks the devil
And he does it fucking well
    With his bloody great, &c.

D

Oh once there was a tinker,
And some folk used to say
He used to ride a charger
Round the country every day.
    With his bloody great kidney wiper
    And his bollocks hanging free
    And yards and yards of foreskin
    Hanging down below his knee,
    Hanging down, hanging down,
    Hanging down, hanging down,
    With yards and yards of foreskin
    Hanging down below his knee.

My lady was a dressing,
A-dressing for a ball,
When she spied that bloody great tinker
Pissing up against her wall.
    With his bloody great, &c.

So she wrote him a letter,
And in it she did say
That she'd rather be fucked by the tinker
Than her husband any day.
    With his bloody great, &c.

The tinker got the letter,
And when it he did read,
Then his prick began to fester,
And his balls began to bleed.
With his bloody great, &c.

So he jumped upon his stallion,
And on it he did ride,
With his penis on the saddle
And his bollocks by his side.
With his bloody great, &c.

He rode up to her mansion,
He rode up to her hall,
'Lord save us,' cried the butler,
'For he's come to fuck us all.'
With his bloody great, &c.

The Mistress in her boudoir,
The servants in the hall,
But the buggering of the butler
Was the dirtiest deed of all.
With his bloody great, &c.

For first he fucked the housemaids,
And then he fucked the wife,
And then he fucked his charger,
And ruined it for life.
With his bloody great, &c.

But now that tinker's dead, Sir,
They say he's gone to hell,
They say he's fucked the Devil,
And I bet he did it well.
With his bloody great, &c.

123. Tobacco

As this poem – from the drollery *Wits Interpreter* (1655) – shows, a sexual identity can be attached to the most unlikely substances.

You that in love do mean to sport,
   Tobacco, tobacco,
Take a wench of the meaner sort,
   Tobacco, tobacco,
But let her have a comely face
Like one that comes of Venus' race,
Then take occasion, time and place
   To give her some tobacco.

Your can with moisture must abound,
   Tobacco, tobacco,
Your bullets must be plump and round,
   Tobacco, tobacco,
Your stopper must be stiff and strong,
Your pipe it must be large and long,
Or else she'll say you do her wrong.
   She'll scorn your weak tobacco.

But if that you do please her well,
   Tobacco, tobacco,
All others then you will excel,
   Tobacco, tobacco,
She will be ready at your call
And take tobacco, pipe and all,
She ready will she be to fall
   To taste your good tobacco.

124. Tradesmen

From *Pills*; note how the catalogue of lasciviousness reaches a crescendo with the tinker (see headnote to No. 122).

O the miller, the dusty musty miller,
  The miller that beareth on his back;
He never goes to measure meal
  But his maid holds ope the sack.

O the baker, the bonny bonny baker,
  The baker that is so full of sin;
He never heats his oven hot
  But he thrusts his maiden in.

O the brewer, the lusty lusty brewer,
  The brewer that brews ale and beer;
He never heats his liquor hot
  But he takes his maid by the gear.

O the butcher, the bloody bloody butcher,
  The butcher that sells both beef and bone;
He never grinds his slaughtering knife
  But his maid must turn his stone.

O the weaver, the wicked wicked weaver,
  That followeth a weary trade;
He never shoots his shuttle right
  But he shoots first at his maid.

O the barber, the neat and nimble barber,
  Whose trade is ne'er the worse;
He never goes to wash and shave
  But he trims his maiden first.

O the tailor, the fine and frisking tailor,
  The tailor that gives so good regard;
He never goes to measure lace
  But his maid holds out his yard.

O the blacksmith, the lusty lusty blacksmith,
   The best of all good fellows;
He never heats his iron hot
   But his maid must blow the bellows.

O the tanner, the merry merry tanner,
   The tanner that draws good hides into leather;
He never strips himself to work
   But his maid and he's together.

O the tinker, the sturdy sturdy tinker,
   The tinker that deals all in mettle;
He never clencheth home a nail
   But his trull holds up the kettle.

125. Twankydillo

Still orally current and unusual in having a chorus longer than the narrative stanza, this has its roots in the seventeenth century.

Here's a health to the merry blacksmith,
The best of good fellows
Who works at the forge
Whilst his maid blows the bellows
  For it makes my great hammer
  To rise and to fall
  Says the young goat to the old goat
  'You're the great goat of all!'
  Twankydillo, twankydillo, twankydillo, dillo, dillo, dillo!
  And he played on his merry bagpipes
  Made from the green willow!

Now if ever I meet with
The shepherd's old wife
I will give her a thrashing
For the rest of her life
  For it makes, &c.

Now if ever I meet with
The shepherd's old horse,
I will cut off the tail
Which covers his arse
  For it makes, &c.

Now if ever I meet with
The shepherd's fair daughter
I will block up the hole
Where she lets out her water
  For it makes, &c.

126. Twins

An early twentieth-century song that owes more to the smutty music-hall manner than to the frankly bawdy popular tradition.

We're the twins, ting-a-ling-a-ling,
The twins, ting-a-ling-a-ling
My brother St John and they know what we're on,
When we're out, there's no doubt,
We're so much alike in our figures and height;
As we stroll along the prom-prom-prom
People shout as we pass:
'There goes six feet of arse.'
It's me and my brother St John.

And it's in with it, out with it, don't fuck about with it,
Glorious gift of the gods;
Women they pray for it,
Brown hatters pay for it –
Knob, glorious knob.

In the summertime we go
To the seaside we go,
The air there's so fresh and it's bracing;
We lie on the sands with our knobs in our hands
Watching the couples embracing,
And whether it's near or whether it's far
People know what we're at and they know who we are

We're the twins, &c.

127. Una's Lock

From *The Giblet Pye* (*c.* 1806); in a letter of September, 1794, Burns referred to it as 'a blackguard Irish song' and added 'I have often regretted the want of decent verses to it that you may sing before Ladies'.

'Twas on a sweet morning
   When violets were a-springing,
The dew the meads adorning,
   The larks melodious singing;
The rose trees, by each breeze,
   Were gently wafted up and down,
And the primrose that then blows
   Bespangled nature's verdant gown.
The purling rill, the murmuring stream,
   Stole gently through the lofty grove:
Such was the time when Darby stole
   Out to meet his barefoot love.

Sweet Una was the tightest,
   Genteelest of the village dames;
Her eyes were the brightest
   That e'er set youthful heart in flames.
Her lover to move her
   By every art in man essayed
In ditty, for pity,
   This lovely maid he often prayed,
But she, perverse, his suit denied.
   Sly Darby, being enraged at this,
Resolved when next they met to seize
   The lock that scatters Una's piss.

Beneath a lofty spreading oak
   She sat with can and milking pail;
From lily hands at each stroke
   In flowing streams the milk did steal.
With peeping, and creeping,
   Sly Darby now comes on apace;

In raptures the youth sees
　　The blooming beauties of her face.
Fired with her charms he now resolved
　　No longer to delay his bliss,
But instantly to catch the lock
　　That scatters pretty Una's piss.

Upon her back he laid her,
　　Turned up her smock so lily white;
With joy the youth surveyed her,
　　Then gaped with wonder and delight.
Her thighs they were so snowy fair,
　　And just between appeared a crack;
The lips red, and overspread
　　With curling hair of jetty black.
Transported now, Darby beholds
　　The sum of all his promised bliss,
And instantly he caught the lock
　　That scatters pretty Una's piss.

Within his arms he seized her,
　　And pressed her to his panting breast;
What more could have appeased her,
　　But oaths which Darby meant in jest.
He swore he'd but adore her,
　　And to her ever constant prove;
He'd wed her, he'd bed her,
　　And none on earth but her he'd love.
With vows like those he won her o'er,
　　And hoped she'd take it not amiss
If he presumed to catch the lock
　　That scatters pretty Una's piss.

His cock it stood erected,
　　His breeches down about his heels,
And what he long expected
　　He now with boundless rapture feels.
Now entered and concentred
　　The beauteous maid lay in a trance,
His bollocks went like elbows
　　Of fiddlers in a country dance.

The melting Una, now she cries,
  'I'd part with life for joy like this';
With showers of bliss they jointly oiled
  The lock that scatters Una's piss.

128. Uncle George

This was popular during the 1920s and doubtless provided light relief from economic adversity.

A

Uncle George and Auntie Mabel
Fainted at the breakfast table,
Now children, let it be a warning
Not to do things in the morning.

Uncle George is much improved
Now he's had his balls removed:
He sits at home and pokes the fire
And sings falsetto in the choir.

B

Uncle George is much improved
Since his balls have been removed:
Now he's free from all desire,
Sings soprano in the choir.

129. Up in the Belfry

The dialect may be a caricature of, rather than a product of, the Yorkshireman; it predates World War One.

Up in 't belfry Verger stands
Pulling pud with horny hands;
Down in 't vestry Vicar yells
'Stop pulling pud, pull 't bloody bells.'

Handsome Butler, buxom Cook,
Down in 't kitchen, having fuck;
Up in 't bedroom Mistress peals
'Stop having fuck, get 't bloody meals.'

130. Vicar

The sexual contest of bawdy tradition is given an ecclesiastical twist in this twentieth-century poem.

A

There once was a vicar of Balham
Who said to his curate John:
'I bet I've had more women than you.'
Said John, 'I'll bet you're wrong, you're wrong.'
Said John, 'I'll bet you're wrong –

We'll both stand outside the church today
And this will be our sign:
You *ding-a-ding* for the women you've had
And I'll *ding-a-dong* for mine, for mine,
I'll *ding-a-dong* for mine.'

There were more *ding-a-dings* than *ding-a-dong-dongs*
Till a pretty young girl walked by
And the curate went *ding-a-dong*.
'Hey,' said the vicar, 'don't *ding-a-dong* there,
That's my wife I do declare.'

'Hell,' said the curate, 'I don't care.'
Ding dong dong-a-dong-a-dong ding dong,
Ding dong dong-a-ding dong.

B

The vicar of a country church
Said to his curate, 'John:
I bet I've fucked more girls than you.'
The curate said, 'You're wrong –

We'll stand at the corner of the church one day
And this shall be our sign:
You'll say *Ding* for the girls you've fucked
And I'll say *Dong* for mine.'

Ding-dong! Ding-dong!

There were many more *Dings* than *Dongs* that day
As the fair young maidens passed that way.
'Hey,' said the vicar, 'don't *Dong* there!
That's my wife I do declare!'
'Balls,' said the curate, 'I don't care.'

Ding-a-ding-ding! Ding-dong!

131. Wake at Kildare

A late nineteenth-century Irish song of seduction still preserved in the oral tradition.

'O mother, darling mother, there's a wake at Kildare,
You know my darling Roger, he's promised to be there;
He loves me, O he loves me, O he loves me for my sake,
O mother, darling mother, may I go to the wake?'

'O Nellie, darling Nellie, beware of Kildare,
I know your darling Roger has promised to be there;
He loves you and he loves you, O he loves you for his sake,
But keep your legs together coming home from the wake.'

Our wee Nellie, as proud as any queen,
She dressed herself in petticoats and drawers so neat and
    clean;
He stuffed her up with whiskey and he stuffed her up with
    cake,
And he stuffed it up wee Nellie coming home from the wake.

Six months passed, nine months passed,
Our wee Nellie, she dropped her load at last;
She hugged it and caressed it and she loved it for its sake
And she called it 'Bastard Barney Coming Home from the
    Wake'.

132. Wanton Seed

This has some thematic affinities with No. 73 and has been current since the nineteenth century; H. E. D. Hammond transcribed a version in 1906.

As I walked out one spring morning fair,
To view the fields and take the air,
There I heard a pretty maid making her complain,
And all she wanted was the chiefest grain, the chiefest grain,
And all she wanted was the chiefest grain.

I said to her, 'My pretty maid,
Come tell me what you stand in need.'
'O yes, kind sir, you're the man to do my deed,
For to sow my meadow with the wanton seed, the wanton
     seed,
For to sow my meadow with the wanton seed.'

Then I sowed high and I sowed low,
And under the bush the seed did grow,
It sprang up so accidentally without any weed,
And she always remembered the wanton seed, the wanton
     seed,
And she always remembered the wanton seed.

133. Wanton Trick

This series of sexual variations on a musical theme is from
Pills.

If anyone long for a musical song
   Although that his hearing be thick,
The sound that it bears will ravish his ears,
   Whoop, 'tis but a wanton trick.

A pleasant young maid on an instrument played,
   That knew neither note nor prick;
She had a good will to live by her skill,
   Whoop, 'tis but a wanton trick.

A youth in that art well seen in his part,
   They called him Derbyshire Dick,
Came to her a suitor and would be her tutor,
   Whoop, 'tis but a wanton trick.

To run with his bow he was not slow,
   His fingers were nimble and quick;
When he played on his bass he ravished the lass,
   Whoop, 'tis but a wanton trick.

He wooed her and taught her until he had brought her
   To hold out a crotchet and prick;
And by his direction she came to perfection,
   Whoop, 'tis but a wanton trick.

With playing and wooing he still would be doing,
   And called her his pretty sweet chick;
His reasonable motion brought her to devotion,
   Whoop, 'tis but a wanton trick.

He pleased her so well that backwards she fell
   And swooned as though she were sick;
So sweet was his note that up went her coat,
   Whoop, 'tis but a wanton trick.

The string of his viol she put to the trial
  Till she had the full length of the stick;
Her white bellied lute she set to his flute,
  Whoop, 'tis but a wanton trick.

Thus she with her lute and he with his flute
  Held every crotchet and prick;
She learned at leisure yet paid for the pleasure,
  Whoop, 'tis but a wanton trick.

His viol string burst her tutor she cursed,
  However she played with the stick;
From October to June she was quite out of tune,
  Whoop, 'tis but a wanton trick.

With shaming her hand to make the pin stand
  The music within her grew thick;
Of his viol and lute appeared some fruit,
  Whoop, 'tis but a wanton trick.

And then she repented that e'er she consented,
  To have either note or prick
For learning so well made her belly to swell,
  Whoop, 'tis but a wanton trick.

All maids that make trial of a lute or a viol
  Take heed how you handle the stick;
If you like not this order come try my recorder,
  Whoop, 'tis but a wanton trick.

And if this ditty forsooth doth not fit ye,
  I know not what music to prick;
There's never a strain but in time will be twain,
  Whoop, 'tis but a wanton trick.

134. Westminster Whore

An early seventeenth-century poem from the Rawlinson MS
(Poet. B.35, leaf 36) it satirises the concept of honour.

As I went to Westminster Abbey
   I saw a young wench on her back,
Cramming in a dildo of tabby
   Into her — till 'twas ready to crack.
'By your leave,' said I, 'pretty maid,
   Methinks your sport is but dry.'
'I can get no better,' she said, 'Sir,
   And I'll tell you the reason why:

Madam P. hath a thing at her breech,
   Sucks up all the scad of the town;
She's a damned lascivious bitch,
   And fucks for half a crown.
Now the curse of a cunt without hair,
   And ten thousand poxes upon her,
We poor whores may go hang in despair,
   We're undone by the Maids of Honour.'

Then in loyalty as I was bound,
   Hearing her speak in this sort,
I fucked her thrice on the ground,
   And bid her speak well of the court.

135. Willing Lover

This poem from the post-Restoration drollery *Wit and Drollery* (1661) ends, unusually, with a dying fall.

She lay up to the navel bare,
   And was a willing lover;
Expecting between hope and fear,
   When I would come and cover.
Her hand beneath my waistband slips,
   To grope in busy wise;
Which caused a trembling in her lips
   And shivering in her eyes.

The blood out of her face did go,
   As it on service went,
To second what was gone before,
   When all its strength was spent.
Her cheeks and lips as coral red,
   Like roses were full blown:
Which fading straight, the leaves were spread,
   And so the prick comes down.

Her breasts then both panting were
   Such comfort wrought between us,
That all the world, I dare to swear,
   Would envy to have seen us.
Her belly and its provender,
   For me was kept in store;
Such news to hear and, not to have share,
   Would have made a man a whore.

Her legs were girt about my waist,
   My hands under her crupper;
As who should say, 'Now break your fast,
   And come again to supper.'
Even as the God of War did knock,
   As any other man will;
For haste of work at twelve o'clock,
   Kept Vulcan at his anvil.

'Mad wag,' quoth she, 'why dost thou make
   Such haste thyself to rear?
Can'st thou not know that for thy sake
   The fair lasts all the year?'
Quiet and calm as are love's streams
   I threw myself about her.
But a pox upon the jests and dreams—
   I had better lain without her.

136. Winnipeg Whore

A twentieth-century (*c.* 1920) Canadian lumberjack's song
which perhaps depicts in details one of the 'Four Old Whores'
of No. 42.

My first trip up the Tipaway River,
My first visit to Canadia's shore,
There I met a Mrs O'Hara
Better known as the Winnipeg Whore.

She comes up and sits right next to me,
Lays her hand upon my knee,
Says 'How's about a little bit of loving then?
Dollar and a half is the usual fee.'

Takes me by the hand and upstairs leads me
To the room where she usually sleeps;
Dirty old room with a straw-filled mattress,
Wasn't too clean but it sure was cheap.

Takes off my hat and my cocky breeches,
Hadn't been in bed for an hour or more
When up jumps the bugger-boys and sons of the bitches
So I ups and I hi-tails out of that door.

So all you sons who sail the ocean
Be on your guard in Canadia's shore:
If you sail up the Tipaway River
Never lay a finger on the Winnipeg Whore.

137. Woodpecker

'Pecker' is a common euphemism for penis which is probably why the woodpecker acquired its sexual identity in this song much enjoyed during World War Two.

I inserted my finger in the woodpecker's hole
And the woodpecker said 'God bless my soul!
Take it out, take it out, take it out,
Withdraw it!'

I withdrew my finger from the woodpecker's hole
And the woodpecker said 'God bless my soul!
Put it back, put it back, put it back,
Replace it!'

I replaced my finger in the woodpecker's hole
And the woodpecker said 'God bless my soul!
Turn it round, turn it round, turn it round,
Revolve it!'

I revolved my finger in the woodpecker's hole
And the woodpecker said 'God bless my soul!
'Tother way, 'tother way, 'tother way,
Reverse it!'

I reversed my finger in the woodpecker's hole
And the woodpecker said 'God bless my soul!
Slow it down, slow it down, slow it down,
Retard it!'

I retarded my finger in the woodpecker's hole
And the woodpecker said 'God bless my soul!
Faster yet, faster yet, faster yet,
I like it!'

138. Woozle

A modern mock-ornithological discourse, possibly the product
of a medical student's imagination.

I've heard of the bird called the Woozle,
The one that lives out in Natal,
And amazes pursuers by flying
Right up its own anal canal.

Remarkable though the position,
It's really strategic for it,
For on to the heads of pursuers
It showers derision and shit.

There once was a Woozle called Willie
Pursued by a man from New York,
Plunging into his spacious cloaca
Misguidedly took the wrong fork.

His blunder was of the first water,
His predicament really appals,
For when he recovered position
He found himself inside his balls.

He wriggled and wiggled and struggled
And started to splutter and cough;
He produced a delightful sensation
And found that he'd tossed himself off.

By now he was feeling lethargic,
In fact was decidedly weak,
So he squeezed through his peritoneum
Emerging once more by his beak.

And that is the reason why Woozles
Often sway as though recently wed,
For they've given up shit and derision
And use spermatozoa instead.

139. Would You Do That?

Collected by Burns and printed in the *c.* 1800 *MMC*, it cleverly avoids the sexual act by a loaded rhetorical question.

Gudewife, when your gudeman's frae hame,
　Might I but be sae bauld,
As come to your bed-chamber,
　When winter nights are cauld;
As come to your bed-chamber
　When nights are cauld and wat,
And lie in your gudeman's stead,
　Wad ye do that?

Young man, an ye should be so kind,
　When our gudeman's frae hame,
As come to my bed-chamber,
　Where I am laid my lane;
And lie in our gudeman's stead,
　I will tell you what,
He fucks me five times ilka night,
　Wad ye do that?

140. Woman's Cunt

A modern example of the sort of poem that circulates by way of MS and typescript rather than by word-of-mouth.

Woman's cunt
  Sweet-dewed benefaction,
Sheath to sword
  Seeking satisfaction;
Woman's lips
  Open ripely,
In cock slips
  Riding tightly;
Woman's tits
  Standing pert,
Proud cock sits
  About to spurt;
Woman's eyes
  Dilate madly,
Man he sighs
  Fucking gladly;
Woman's bum
  Squeezes member,
Milks his come
  To cool her ember;
Woman's mouth
  Honeyed pot,
North to south
  Draws his shot;
Woman's legs
  Drawn up
Have juice begs
  Cock to sup;
Woman's mound
  Silken-haired,
Jerking sound
  As love's declared;
Woman groaned
  As man's hot seed
All sins atoned
  Fulfilled her need.

141. Yellow Yellow Yorlin'

A song – collected by Burns and printed in the *c.* 1800 *MMC* – that extends the sexually symbolic nest-image (see headnote to No. 31).

It fell on a day, in the flow'ry month o' May,
   All on a merry merry mornin',
I met a pretty maid, an' unto her I said,
   'I wad fain fin' your yellow yellow yorlin'.'   *finch*

'O no, young man,' says she, 'you're a stranger to me,
   An' I am anither man's darlin',
Wha has baith sheep an' cows, that's feedin' in the hows,
   An' a cock for my yellow yellow yorlin'.'

'But, if I lay you down upon the dewy ground,
   You wad nae be the waur ae farthing;   *worse*
An' that happy, happy man, he never wou'd ken
   That I play'd wi' your yellow yellow yorlin'.'

'O fie, young man,' says she, 'I pray you let me be,
   I wad na for five pound sterling;
My mither wad gae mad, an' sae wad my dad,
   If you play'd wi' my yellow yellow yorlin'.'

But I took her by the waist, an' laid her down in haste,
   For a' her squakin' and squalin';
The lassie soon grew tame, an' bade me come again
   For to play wi' her yellow yellow yorlin'.'

142. Ye'se Get a Hole to Hide It In

A song – collected by Burns and printed in the *c.* 1800 *MMC* – counselling sexual patience.

O will ye speak at our town,
    As ye come frae the fair?
An' ye'se get a hole to hide it in,
    Ye'se get a hole to hide it in;
Will ye speak at our town
    As ye come frae the fair,
Ye'se get a hole to hide it in,
    Will haud it a' and mair.

O haud awa your hand, Sir,
    Ye gar me ay think shame;
An' ye'se get a hole to hide it in;
    Ye'se get a hole to hide it in;
O haud awa your hand, Sir,
    Ye gar me ay think shame;
An' ye'se get a hole to hide it in,
    An' think yoursel at hame.

O will ye let abee, Sir;
    Toots! now, ye've rivt my sark,
An' ye'se get a hole to hide it in,
    Ye'se get a hole to hide it in;
O will ye let abee, Sir;
    Toots! now, ye've reft my sark;
An' ye'se get a hole to hide it in,
    Whar ye may work your wark.

O haud awa your hand, Sir,
    Ye're like to pit me daft;
An' ye'se get a hole to hide it in,
    Ye'se get a hole to hide it in;
O haud awa your hand, Sir,
    Ye're like to put me daft;
An' ye'se get a hole to hide it in,
    To keep it warm and saft.

O had it in your hand, Sir,
    Till I get up my claes,
An' ye'se get a hole to hide it in,
    Ye'se get a hole to hide it in;
O had it in your hand, Sir,
    Till I get up my claes;
An' ye'se get a hole to hide it in,
    To keep it frae the flaes.

flies

248

143. Young and Old Women

This poem from an eighteenth-century MS in the National Library of Scotland (19.3.16) explores the ancient theme of faded beauty.

Young women to the dancing schools repair
Where, with fond gestures, poor men to ensnare.
And, when they're old, and no more fit to catch
They go to church but first they paint and patch.
They wish and pray that man would take the hint,
When one they eye, t'others look a squint.
And thus religion's turned into a farce
Only to gain a lusty standing tarse.

144. Young Man of Brighton Pier

Perhaps the finest of the teasing-rhyme variety of bawdy poem, this twentieth-century effort comes complete with a happy ending of domestic bliss.

One very hot day in the summer last year
A young man was seen swimming round Brighton Pier;
He dived underneath it and swam to a rock
And amused all the ladies by shaking his
Fist at a copper who stood on the shore,
The very same copper who copped him before.

For the policeman to order him out was a farce,
For the cheeky young man simply showed him his
Graceful manoeuvres and wonderful pace
And when once ashore only laughed in his face.

This young man and his sweetheart would go for a swim
And travel some way with his hand on her
Chest to support her should she feel tired,
A kindly attention the lady admired.

He'd swim like a drake and she like a duck,
Then finish the morning by having a
Nice little lunch and a bottle of wine,
A treat which no lady was known to decline.

Her dress made of serge was the nicest of fits
And showed to advantage the swell of her
Graceful figure from her head to her feet;
Her appearance, in fact, was exceedingly neat.

While he lounged on the beach she started to hunt
For some lovely seaweed to hang round her
Window at home, a reminder to be
Of the happy long hours she had spent by the sea.

If for a moment his lady he'd miss
He'd wager his life she was doing a

Kind thoughtful action, by kiss or caress
Soothing some poor little child in distress.

To return to the story – when evening falls
She pleases her boyfriend by tickling his
Fancy with yarns how for the rest of her life
She'll be to her darling his dear little wife.

He fervently blesses the day he was born,
And all through her kissing he's now got the
Idea in his head that he can't live alone
And as soon as he can he must set up a home.

Note on the text

Unless otherwise indicated in the headnotes the texts are traditional and I would like to thank the following for communicating material to me: Alex Bridge, J. P. Bridger, Cedric Boam, Geoffrey Brown, T. Christie, Paddy Clark, Adam Cohen, Neil Fenton, Alan Grant, C. I. C. Harrison-Wallace, D. W. Hutchings, Forbes MacGregor, P. Motte-Harrison, S. W. Nelki, Tom Scott, Drew Snider, John Wiseman. Three abbreviations are used in the headnotes: Legman is Gershon Legman's indispensable study of erotica *The Horn Book* (New York 1964); *MMC* is *The Merry Muses of Caledonia* which exists in several editions hence the emphasis on date of publication; *Pills* is Thomas D'Urfey's *Wit and Mirth; or Pills to Purge Melancholy* (6 vols., 1719–20). Purists may object to the omission of musical illustration but I wanted to present, to a wide public, the primary textual material. Some of the pieces are tuneless recitations and, as far as rural bawdry is concerned, I agree with Legman (p. 407) that 'the basic activity of folksong is not that of the musician but that of the poet'. Music is, of course, a useful mnemonic device and in time bawdry, like balladry, may get its Bronson. Meanwhile some of the items (Nos. 12B, 13, 14, 30, 31, 33, 41B, 63, 77, 80, 121, 122B) can be heard, as performed by skilled folksingers, on *Songs of Seduction* (Topic Records 1961, 12T 158). There is also an excellent Australian recording of bawdy songs, including a fine rendering of 'Eskimo Nell': *The "R" Certificate Song Book* (Balwyn, Victoria, 2 vols., R1 and R2). For future editions of this book I would be delighted to receive fresh contributions from the general public: either new examples of bawdry or variants of items included in the anthology. I can be reached via Sphere Books.

Index of first lines

A selection of Bestsellers from Sphere Books

Fiction

SHARKY'S MACHINE	William Diehl	£1.75	☐
THE LAST CATTLE DRIVE	Robert Day	95p	☐
VIXEN 03	Clive Cussler	£1.25	☐
THE DEATH FREAK	Clifford Irving & Herbert Berkholz	95p	☐
WOLFSBANE	Craig Thomas	£1.25	☐
PLANTATION	Maurice Denuziere	£1.50	☐
SEASON OF PASSION	Danielle Steel	£1.25	☐

Film and TV Tie-ins

THE PROFESSIONALS 5: BLIND RUN	Ken Blake	85p	☐
THE PROFESSIONALS 6: FALL GIRL	Ken Blake	85p	☐
THE PROMISE	Danielle Steel	95p	☐
BUCK ROGERS IN THE 25TH CENTURY	Addison E. Steele	95p	☐
BUCK ROGERS 2: THAT MAN ON BETA	Addison E. Steele	95p	☐

Non-Fiction

THE THIRD WORLD WAR	General Sir John Hackett	£1.75	☐
EVEREST: IMPOSSIBLE VICTORY	Peter Habeler	£1.50	☐
THE HURRICATS	Ralph Barker	£1.25	☐
LEGACY OF THE GODS	Robert Charroux	£1.50	☐

All Sphere books are available at your local bookshop or newsagent, or can be ordered direct from the publisher. Just tick the titles you want and fill in the form below.

Name...

Address..

....

Write to Sphere Books, Cash Sales Department, P.O. Box 11, Falmouth, Cornwall TR10 9EN.

Please enclose cheque or postal order to the value of the cover price plus:

UK: 25p for the first book plus 10p per copy for each additional book ordered to a maximum charge of £1.05.

OVERSEAS: 40p for the first book and 12p for each additional book.

BFPO & EIRE: 25p for the first book plus 10p per copy for the next 8 books, thereafter 5p per book.

Sphere Books reserve the right to show new retail prices on covers, which may differ from those previously advertised in the text or elsewhere, and to increase postal rates in accordance with the GPO.

(10:79)